THE LAND OF CHRISTMAS

THE LAND OF

Text by Mary Phraner Warren

SPCK London

CHRISTMAS

Nineteenth-century engravings and drawings

THE LAND OF CHRISTMAS

First published 1979
SPCK
Holy Trinity Church
Marylebone Road
London NW1 4DU

Text — Augsburg Publishing House, Minneapolis, Minnesota.
Design, layout, and illustrations — Sadan Publishing House.

Picture research by Yishai Afek
Art coloring and design by Tova Kleiner

Manufactured by Sadan Publishing House Ltd.,
1 David Hamelech St., Tel Aviv, Israel

ISBN 0 281 03701 9

Contents

Acknowledgments

I would like to thank Beth Israel Congregation, Augustana Lutheran Church, Warner Pacific College, and University of Portland for opening their libraries to me. I extend my thanks to Dr. Robert Boyd, who spent many hours reading the manuscript and giving valuable criticism.

It is important for the reader to realize that biblical scholars and historians and archeologists differ widely on many of the details I have included in my book. The descriptions of the Temple as it was reconstructed by Herod are so numerous, so complex, and so varied, for instance, that I found it necessary to lean heavily on one or two sources (especially Joan Comay's *The Temple of Jerusalem)* instead of attempting to piece together conflicting information.

Preface

Whether or not we grew up in a Christian community, many of us know the Christmas story by heart. We are so familiar with the beautiful prose of Matthew and Luke that we seldom realize how many details are missing. It is easy to accept without question the Sunday school rendition of Christmas, complete with gilded coat-hanger halos and gauze angel wings. There is nothing wrong with a lovingly planned pageant, nothing wrong with the familiar figures of the creche, be they life-sized or tiny enough to hold in the palm of a hand. But how do we discover what the first Christmas was really like?

We cannot say for certain that Mary rode to Bethlehem on the back of the family donkey. We know, however, that first-century Jewish families did use donkeys for both work and travel. No record tells how many Wise Men came from afar to offer gifts, or what routes Mary and Joseph took on their journeys, or where they settled in Egypt, or what they did while they were there. But through the years archeologists and historians have provided material concerning the clothing and food and daily life and customs of Jewish families of that era. In piecing these bits of information together into a giant puzzle, we can only say that much of it is contained within the Old and New Testaments; much is conjecture based on a careful study of the days when Jesus lived on earth.

Why a book about the land of Christmas? If the land becomes real, perhaps the people who lived and worked and worshiped there will turn out to be human beings like ourselves, instead of costumed characters in a play.

And so it is our hope that this book will serve as a guide to more meaningful celebration of the most joyful event ever recorded in human history.

Title page: Jerusalem, from the Mount of Olives

Overleaf: Reading Holy Scripture, with Gaza in the background

THE LAND WHERE CHRISTMAS HAPPENED

Palestine
in the
Time of Our
Sidon
SYRIA
Tyre
Dan
Caesarea Philippi
Kadesh
Gennesareth
Capernaum
Carmel
Cana
Tiberias
GALILEE
ITUREA
Gadara
Nazareth
Nain
Endor
Pella
Caesare
Gilboa
Jabesh Gilead
Succoth
Samaria
Gilgal
SAMARIA
Jacobs Well
Ramoth Gilead
Saron
Shiloh
Joppa
Bethel
Arimathea
Rabbath Ammon
Emmaus
Rama
PEREA
Jerusalem
Jericho
Nebo
Heshbon
Olivet
Azotus
Bethlehem
JUDEA
Ascalon
Dibon
Hebron
Engedi
Gaza
MOAB
Beersheba
Aroer
Ramath
GREAT SEA
MEDITERRANEAN

"And I will give to you, and to your descendants after you, the land of your sojournings." **Genesis 17:8**

The land of God's Chosen People was, and still is, a small spot on the globe. A land of rugged steppes, mountains and valleys, canyons and deserts, vineyards, wheat and barley fields, rocky pastures, and mile upon endless mile of thorny, barren waste — that is Christmas land.

Centuries before Jesus was born in Bethlehem, God had promised Abraham and his descendants a holy land. The first five books of the Old Testament call the promised land Canaan. As tribes migrated and fought, the territory expanded, but no single name covered the southern part, Judah, and the northern part, Israel. At the time of David the united kingdom became known as Israel. Greek navigators referred to one strip along the southern coast as the land of the *Palaestini* or Philistines. It was after the introduction of Christianity that the entire area became known as Palestine.

Palestine is no bigger than the state of Vermont or the country of Wales. Yet, because it forms a crucial land bridge between the continents of Asia and Africa, people have fought to control this region since the dawn of history.

On the west, Palestine is bordered by the Mediterranean Sea, and on the east by another natural boundary, the Syro-Arabian desert. The Lebanon and Anti-Lebanon mountain ranges loom to the north, with the snowy peak of Mt. Hermon towering in the distance. To the south, below the Dead Sea and Beersheba, lie Idumaea, where Herod was born, and desert country.

In addition to being strategically located as a land bridge, Palestine forms part of the great curve of rich earth, stretching between the sea and desert and mountains, known as the Fertile Crescent. Far back in geological time, two gigantic faults cut through the region. The land sank, forming a deep, trenchlike valley running north and south. Through it the Jordan River twists and turns.

Left: Embroidered map of the Holy Land, 19th century, England, anonymous

When Jesus lived, the country was made up of four regions. The first consisted of three maritime plains. To the south, between Joppa and Gaza, was the Plain of Philistia. The fertile Plain of Sharon extended from the hills of Samaria to the seacoast. The Plain of Acre (Acco), north of Carmel, was a narrow strip of sandy coastline. Between the Plain of Philistia and the high central mountainous range lay the low hills known as the *Shephelah* or lowlands.

The second area was a series of steppes alternating with very narrow gorges. Beyond them was the high country. Many have called this stretch of ridges and hills the backbone of Palestine. The high country has no towering peaks like the Rockies or the Alps, but the contrast of hill with steep gorge and plain has always left the indelible impression of mountainous terrain.

In the southern part of the high country were the hills and ravines of Judea. Judea included the craggy, uninhabitable cliffs along the Dead Sea, as well as the wild, mysterious wilderness area which provided a background for famous biblical scenes.

To the north of Judea was Samaria. Here a mixed group of people interpreted Jewish law differently. Devout Jews considered them heretics and therefore unclean and avoided them whenever possible.

Above Samaria lay the fertile, hilly province of Galilee where Jesus lived as a boy. Judean Jews were suspicious of these Galilean people. They were descendants of the foreigners who had moved in long ago when the faithful had been exiled to Babylonia. Only 100 years before the birth of Jesus, Galilee was united with Judea by Aristobulus, a Maccabean ruler who gave the people living there a choice: they must be circumcised according to the ancient law, or they must leave. The full name of this area, *Galil-ha-goyim,* means "region of the Gentiles." Judean Jews mocked Galileans because of their heavy accent and because, compared with the austere existence of Jews in the barren south, life in the fertile province of Galilee seemed soft indeed.

Right: The wilderness on the borders of Edom, south of the Dead Sea

The third major area of Palestine was the immense cleavage through which the Jordan River twisted from the foothills of Mt. Hermon into Lake Galilee and south. The earth knows no deeper rift than this. Along the river was a luxuriant strip of tropical growth. Farther along, where the rift was deepest, the river wound down and emptied at last into that strange salty body of water, the Dead Sea. The abrupt descent from Jerusalem, 2500 feet above sea level, to the Dead Sea, nearly 1300 feet below sea level, was almost 3800 feet. Beyond the desolate slopes of this area was wilderness.

The fourth section of Palestine, on the outer edge, was Bedouin country — a mountainous plateau to the east and the land of the Edomites, Idumaea, to the south. Far beyond the steppes lay the majestic hills of Moab. Moses had gazed on the promised land from these hills and Ruth had spent her childhood there.

The climate of Palestine was similar to that of the rest of the Mediterranean area. A dry season began as early as March and extended through most of September. The variable rainy season lasted from mid-October until March or later. Some years there was rain as late as May. At first gentle rains softened the baked earth. Then came storms so violent that boats caught in the middle of the little Lake of Galilee were easily capsized. December, January, and February were the months of the torrential rains. Between summer and winter were an autumn and spring so brief they could not be considered separate seasons.

We are not certain about the date of Christmas. Jesus may have been born in the spring after the torrential rains had ceased. Some historians believe it unlikely that Joseph and Mary traveled from Nazareth to Bethlehem when heavy rains were expected. Many spots along the way would have been impassable, whatever route they took. And, during winter months, Judea was dreary and cold.

In such bad weather, shepherds would be grazing their flocks near home where shelter was available. According to the biblical account, they were out in the fields on a clear and starry night when the angels brought the joyous news of the holy birth.

A thorny branch from the Judean mountains

Right: A fountain in the wilderness at Ein Gedi

Water was scarce throughout most of the Holy Land. From ancient times, the Hebrew people had terraced the hillsides to keep winter rains from washing the earth away, and to catch as much water as possible for their crops. They carved cisterns in the soft limestone rock, too, to hold a more permanent water supply. Lucky were those who lived near a spring, for water was cherished in the land of the Chosen People.

The psalmist praised God by singing, "Thou makest springs gush forth in the valleys; they flow between the hills" (Ps. 104:10).
And Isaiah spoke longingly of water over and over again, promising the faithful a time when:

waters shall break forth in the wilderness,
and streams in the desert;
the burning sand shall become a pool,
and the thirsty ground springs of water;
the haunt of jackals shall become a swamp,
the grass shall become reeds and rushes (Isa. 35:6-7).

Today, much of Palestine is being irrigated and reclaimed. Places once uninhabited are flourishing with kibbutzim and factories, orchards and farms.

When the events of the Christmas story took place, oaks were common as well as the terebinth or turpentine tree and the carob with its long pods. Around the Lake of Galilee, sometimes called Gennesaret, laurel grew in profusion. If the holy birth did occur in spring, creamy laurel flowers would have been in bloom when Mary and Joseph set out to go to Bethlehem. The olive tree grew everywhere, as did the fig, providing beautiful leafy shade against the scorching rays of the sun. Apricot, almond, and pomegranate trees were common.

Palestine was known for its luscious grapes. The symbol of the vine is used many times throughout the Bible. Cereal grains such as wheat, millet, and barley (which the poor used most of the time for bread) grew especially well on some of the plains.

We may be surprised to realize how few Jews lived in the Holy Land at the time of Jesus' birth. Scattered here and there were fewer than two million, according to several historians. For centuries the Hebrew people had watched the conquerors come and go — Egyptians, Assyrians, Babylonians, Persians, Greeks, and now the Romans.

Palms, grapes, and fruit of the Holy Land

There were signs of Greek and Roman influence throughout the land, in spite of protests by rabbis. Hebrew was no longer spoken except in cultivated Jewish circles and in the synagogue and school. Instead, the Jewish inhabitants of Palestine used Aramaic as their primary language. *Koine,* the Hellenistic Greek of the time, was used by those who were better educated.

The influence of Greek art and architecture was clearly seen, particularly in cities of the Decapolis on the shore of Lake Galilee. But in many places Roman generals had carted statues and other treasures home to Italy.

The Romans were beginning to construct their magnificently engineered roads, but most of the best roads would not be finished for years to come. The Jews, especially the wealthy, could benefit greatly from good roads. Travel would be simplified. It would be easier to get supplies from distant places, and there would be more variety in fruits and spices, fine cloth, cosmetics, and perfumes.

In parts of the Holy Land people had little quarrel with this new Roman rule. The Idumaeans and the Samaritans had been converted to Judaism only after defeat in violent wars. They hoped to prosper by cooperating with the Roman emperor. One Idumaean prince lusted for power and thought it wise to remain on good terms with the conquerors. His name was Herod the Great.

Olives and pomegranates

Jews living in Galilee and Judea chafed under the heavy taxes imposed by Rome. They had religious differences with one another, but they were united on one matter: They despised the Roman oppressors. How could they obey Roman law and pay homage to a foreign emperor when the *Torah* was their law, and the Lord, not Caesar, their ruler and king?

The Chosen People loved their tiny, rugged land as much as they loved their children. For hundreds of years they had been sojourners in it and, at times, deported to other places. Often they had fed on "the bread of tears" (Ps. 80:5).

They looked for the promised Messiah as the one who would deliver them from foreign oppressors. For most Jews, regaining the Holy Land was far more important than the person of the deliverer. Some had grown weary and fainthearted through difficult years. But the faithful continued to gather each Sabbath, exultant and full of hope. Nobody could say when the great day would arrive.

And then it happened! — quietly, without trumpets or fanfare. The angel Gabriel announced to a peasant girl named Mary that the Word of God, written for centuries on the hearts of his Chosen People, would be made flesh and dwell among them. She would bear a holy child!

Right: Bethlehem, the town of the nativity

NAZARETH, HOME OF MARY

"In the sixth month the angel Gabriel was sent from God to a city of Galilee named Nazareth, to a virgin betrothed to a man whose name was Joseph." **Luke 1:26-27**

Cupped in the limestone hills of lower Galilee was the small town where Mary lived when Gabriel appeared to her. The Bible provides no details about Nazareth. It is not mentioned once in the Old Testament. Located near the northern border of the Plain of Jezreel, about 15 miles from the Lake of Galilee, Nazareth was a town of little importance. Other towns such as nearby Jotapata and the busy Greek city of Sepphoris several miles to the north were better known and closer to the trade routes. Sepphoris, in fact, was located on the main route which bypassed Nazareth and ran from Ptolemais to Tiberias.

Nazareth could boast of no special industry. It was simply a peaceful dwelling place for farmers and craftsmen, and for shepherds who grazed their flocks above the terraced slopes.

The town was nestled into a valley, and the view from the surrounding foothills was breathtaking. In one direction stretched the golden Plain of Jezreel (Esdraelon), and beyond it, gleaming in sunlight, the distant blue Mediterranean. Turning toward the north and northeast, one could see faraway mountains, with the snowy peak of Mt. Hermon overshadowing them all. There were caravan routes, the many little houses and buildings of various cities and towns, and the deep valley of the Jordan River, a jagged scar on the landscape.

After heavy winter rains, when trees leafed out and the hillsides were green, flowers bloomed everyplace. There were anemone, narcissus, the small wild crocus, and fragrant hyacinth. Beautiful shrubs such as the oleander were in bloom and the clear air was filled with the twitter of birds.

Nazareth was blessed with an adequate supply of water. At the edge of town was a spring where the women and young girls

Previous page: A well at Nazareth

Left: Flowers from the shores of the Sea of Galilee

gathered daily to fill their jugs. Cisterns carved out of the soft white limestone caught rainwater for future use.

At the time of Gabriel's visit, Mary was probably about 15 years of age. It was customary for a Jewish father to select a future husband for his daughter while she was very young, and Mary had already been promised to Joseph, a village carpenter.

Once the promise was made and sealed, sometimes in writing but often only verbally, the girl remained in the home of her parents until the wedding took place about a year later. The betrothal was legally binding. The consequences were dire if it was discovered that a girl had been unfaithful to her future husband. Neighbors would make her drink a bitter concoction containing dust from the floor of the Temple. If she became ill, she would be considered guilty and they would be compelled to follow the ancient law, taking her out to the gate of the town and stoning her to death.

A man was allowed to cancel the betrothal vow by giving his espoused wife a letter of divorcement. If he happened to die before his wedding day, the bride-to-be would be a widow, exactly as if the marriage had already taken place.

We do not know where Mary was when Gabriel startled her. She may have been in her family's dwelling, or sitting on the rooftop. The women and young girls spent most of their time at home.

They had grain to grind into flour, flat, pancakelike loaves to shape and bake, small brothers and sisters to watch, perhaps a pile of wool or some flax to spin into thread. It was no disgrace for men to ply the loom, but only women used the distaff and spindle, which was a round shank of wood with a hook at the top to catch the wool or flax.

Houses were set close together, for the sake of safety, along the narrow, crooked dirt streets. A few homes might have had several rooms around a courtyard, but most were small square blocks of limestone. Where limestone was not abundant, people built homes of clay shaped into bricks and dried in the sun.

Right: Closely packed houses in Shunem below Mt. Gilboa, much as ancient villages stood

Often there was no window. The narrow door opened into a small, enclosed courtyard. Some homes were built against a natural limestone cave and the cave was incorporated as extra living quarters.

At the right side of the door was a little case, the *Mezuzah,* containing the commandments of God.

Livestock occupied the floor of the dwelling. At the rear, a narrow set of stone steps led to the platform where the family slept. Furniture was sparse. The beds were usually woven reed mats, unrolled at night and set side by side so the family could share whatever covering was available — a heavy cloak or a blanket. Jesus later told a parable about a man who could not get up and answer the knock on his door in the middle of the night because he would awaken his family. He would have had to climb over them!

Inclement weather meant that meals had to be served on the platform, but whenever possible food was cooked and eaten outside. Mealtimes were casual unless a feast had been planned.

A few homes might have had low tables, but most families sat on the floor. Houses seldom had fireplaces, although some families owned a little charcoal brazier for warmth in cooler weather. Ordinarily they cooked over an open fire which was set between two stones in a place hollowed out in the ground.

Right: Fashionable Israelite house — a partly covered oblong court with rooms leading off on three sides. Furniture was simple. Pottery vessels were stored in wall niches. The roof was of beams and closely packed mud. (Reconstruction)

First century oil lamp

Some of the people owned a small clay oven, but often dough was carried in a wooden trough to the communal oven. At other times it was slapped into flat rounds and baked on a metal sheet set over the open fire, much the way we make pancakes today.

Humble homes had but one lamp, a round or oval flat piece of clay with an earlike handle pinched out at one end. The lamp

contained a hole where the wick was set, and a second hole for olive oil. While burning, it filled the small dark home with an oily, sweetish smell. It was kept lit even at night when the family slept.

According to tradition, Mary was born in Jerusalem to Joachim and Anne. Nothing is known about her childhood. Jewish men were proud of their women and far more kind to girl babies than were other Middle Eastern cultures. Boy babies certainly were preferred and girls were often considered a burden, but it would not cross a father's mind to follow the pagan custom of leaving a girl baby on a hillside to die of exposure. In the first place, it was against Jewish law. In the second place, Jews were very fond of children. Barrenness was considered shameful.

Close to Nazareth, the country had been affected by the ways of Greece and Rome. But homes in Nazareth probably had none of the conquerors' frills. The townspeople were orthodox Jews who believed it unclean to bend to pagan ways.

Mary would not have attended the primary school in her synagogue. Some rabbis could not see any sense in teaching the *Torah* to girls, but others thought it wise to do so. From the ancient hymns Mary sang as a young woman, it seems likely that she had been lovingly taught the Scriptures by her parents at home.

Mary probably wore the loose-belted robe or dress (often called a "coat" in translation) common in her day. Because she was a woman, she would not have worn tassels dangling from the hem of this garment. The law forbade mixing two different types of cloth, such as wool and flax. Her robe may have been made of either one of these materials, but not a combination.

Sometimes the cloth was bleached as white as snow. Frequently it was dyed beautiful colors. The dyes were made from the roots and bark and flowers of native plants. Often, too, the clothing was embroidered.

Right: Open stairway on a Bethlehem house; women grinding corn

Mary's home may have had a wooden chest or two where linens and extra robes could be stored.

First century wedding ring and necklace

Right: Carrying water from a well

Overleaf: The mountains of Judea, on the way to Ein Kerem

In the household chest would be stored head coverings, large pieces of cloth which could be tied so the folds would fall gracefully over the forehead. Women seem to have worn their head coverings loosely, rather like a large veil.

Mary probably loved jewelry and perfume. Eastern women often adorned their persons with rings — earrings and finger rings and toe rings. Men and women were permitted to wear such finery, although the stricter rabbis frowned on too much of it and the law forbade piercing of nose or ears.

The people of Nazareth walked about barefoot much of the time. Nobody wore shoes inside a house. Sandals were common, but Mary may have carried hers much of the time so they would last longer.

Jewish women were not required to fulfill duties scheduled for a set time, such as reciting the *Shema* or reading the Law. At synagogue Mary joined the other women and girls sitting behind a special latticework in a section removed from the men.

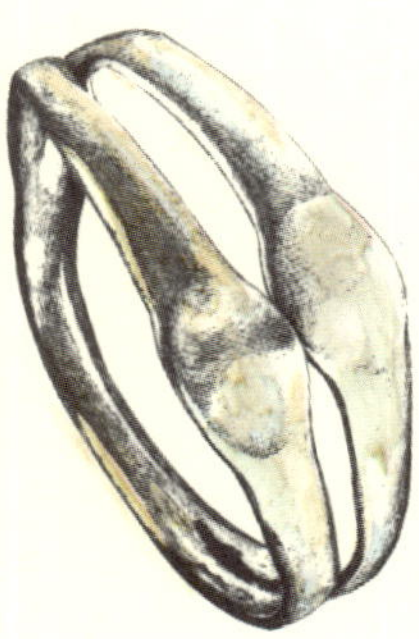

Mary realized she would be considered the property of her husband. But she must have known, too, that Joseph would treat her kindly and respect her for her contribution to the life of their home.

Life in Galilee had its problems. At times the winter rains might destroy a home or several homes at once. More often it was at least necessary to repair the roof with fresh branches and clay, rolling it carefully with a special tool. People had to face the horrors of leprosy, birth defects, blindness, poverty. But certainly it was less arduous to eke out an existence from the red fertile earth in this northern province than in Judea or other parts of Palestine.

Yet Mary decided to leave her home for a few months and to journey into the stark hills of that rugged province where her cousin Elizabeth lived. She longed to share her news with someone who might understand. And the angel had said that Elizabeth, an older woman, would also bear a child!

JOURNEY TO JUDEA

"In those days Mary arose and went with haste into the hill country, to a city of Judah." **Luke 1:39**

Did Mary confide in Joseph before she left Nazareth or when she returned? We have no record. On the one hand, a betrothed young Jewish woman of the first century seldom had much contact with her future husband until the wedding day. On the other hand, Mary was leaving so abruptly she may have felt it necessary to explain to Joseph and her family. She would have had to persuade them of the importance of her journey since, according to Jewish custom, a betrothed virgin was not supposed to travel.

We can only guess at the worrisome thoughts crowding Mary's mind. By the time she returned from Judea, neighbors probably would be able to see that she was carrying a child. And when the gossip started, she must have dreaded what would happen next. If she convinced Joseph and her family it would be good for her to be absent from Nazareth for a time, they could think the matter over and decide what must be done.

Mary's mother may have helped her pack food for the journey, enough bread and a cake or two of dried figs and other fruits, perhaps some goat cheese. At the well outside Nazareth she would have filled her goatskin bag with water.

We do not know whether she borrowed the family's donkey or went on foot. And there is no record of the route she took. One road led south through the Jordan Valley, but it had serious drawbacks. In some places a traveler had to go 12 or 15 miles through sun-scorched land before reaching the next waterhole. During the arid season, the midday heat was far too severe to permit travel. At night bandits lurked in the wildest places.

It is likely that she traveled in a group, possibly a passing caravan or maybe two caravans which joined each other along the way. In the company of a caravan, Mary could have gone this way to the home of Elizabeth. It is far more likely that she took the well-

Left: A natural bridge in front of a vast cavern

traveled route along the central ridges to the west of the Jordan River. The ridge road had a different drawback, but it was one that could be faced. It traversed the hated province of Samaria. Here, in some of the valleys, there was also the danger of being set upon by bandits.

It was a three-day journey from Galilee to Jerusalem. Mary might have been on the road for part of another day too, taking a side footpath into the hill country where Zacharias and Elizabeth lived.

Judea was a small, thin strip of land, half of which was desert. Except for Jerusalem, set on the crest of two hills cut through by a valley, there were no sizable cities or towns. By modern standards, even the Holy City was not a metropolis. Historians have reckoned its population during the time of Jesus to have numbered between 50,000 and 150,000.

Terrace cultivation typical of farming methods in Judea

Jackals, whose melancholy cry, starting at sunset and never ceasing till sunrise, is very distressing

The north-south road Mary probably traveled ran along the high broken limestone ridge through the center of Judea. In addition to Jerusalem, several smaller towns — Bethlehem, Hebron, and Beersheba — were situated along this route, protected by the shelter of the steep slopes. The route followed the waterholes. From ancient times, wherever a watering place could be found, there was usually a settlement.

If a traveler happened to discover a waterhole a few miles off the main route, word got around and a foot track was soon worn in that direction.

In any inhabited spot Mary would have seen terraced hillsides with fruit trees and vineyards, a welcome sight after mile upon mile of lonely hill and valley. Surely she felt to her very bones the solitude of the vast, thorny, barren country stretching before her. The few trees were scrubby and small, casting meager shadows. The bare hills were sliced by deep ravines. This was the parched and thirsty land mentioned throughout the Bible.

In the cooler part of the day lizards skittered from the rocks. Now and then a vulture soared in the brilliant blue sky overhead. At night wolves howled from the hillsides. There were jackals, too.

The vulture

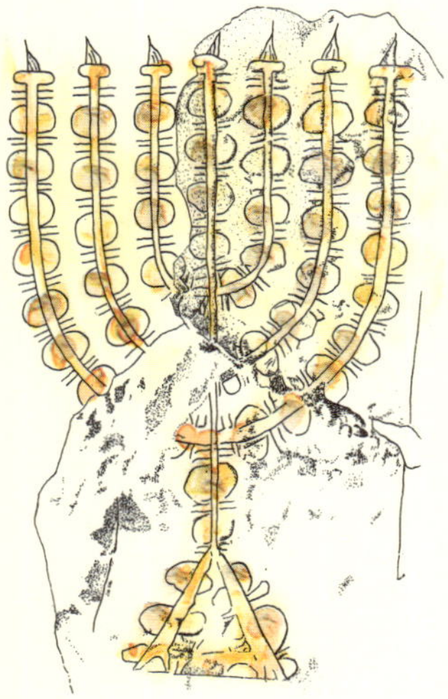

In a secluded valley in the hill country a few miles west of Jerusalem was the village of Ein Kerem. Tradition dating from the fourth century held this to be the home of Zacharias and Elizabeth. They were of the blood of Aaron. A pious Jewish couple, they had reached old age without a child. The expected son was thought to be a miraculous blessing.

Zacharias was one of 20,000 priests in the Holy Land. The priests were allowed to live away from Jerusalem but had to travel to the Holy City when it was their group's turn to serve for a week in the Temple. Zacharias, of the group of Abia, had been on duty when he, like Mary, received a visit from Gabriel.

The priests were assigned to many different tasks. They helped prepare beasts for sacrifice, cleaned the holy vessels, sounded the trumpets, and examined people for signs of leprosy. For the most coveted jobs, lots were drawn to avoid petty jealousy.

Offering incense on the altar was thought to be the holiest of all tasks. It was such an honor that a priest was allowed to do it only once during his lifetime. After he had served in this capacity he would no longer draw lots.

Two assistants would have been chosen to help Zacharias prepare the altar, one to clear away ashes from the last day's sacrifice, the other to place fresh burning coals on the altar. Then Zacharias would have entered alone to wait for the signal to spread incense on the hot coals.

Twelve steps led to the porch of the sanctuary. A gate opened into it. The sanctuary was divided into two parts. In the Holy Place was the seven-branched candelabra of shining gold on the left, and the Table of Showbread on the right. Between them was the Golden Altar of Incense.

Hidden behind a heavy veil was the entrance to the Most Holy Place. Only the high priest, in his ornate blue embroidered robe and special ephod, was allowed to enter there.

Contemporary drawing of Jerusalem Temple's sacred Menorah (candelabrum). Found by archeologists in a first century house.

Overleaf: Nazareth, looking toward the Plain of Esdraelon

During the rite, while the people were praying, the angel appeared. Trembling in astonishment, the old priest asked for a sign. "Behold," Gabriel told him, "you will be silent and unable to speak until the day that these things come to pass, because you did not believe my words, which will be fulfilled in their time" (Luke 1:20). Zacharias was still without speech when Mary came to visit.

Delighted to see Mary, Elizabeth greeted the young woman warmly. In Luke's account she seems to have recognized immediately the connection between the two births.

We have no other information about this visit. We know only that Mary, ecstatically joyful, sang a hymn similar to the ones found in the Old Testament. It would be sung through the coming centuries also, in Christian churches throughout the world:

My soul magnifies the Lord,
and my spirit rejoices in God my Savior,
for he has regarded the low estate of
his handmaiden.
For behold, henceforth all generations will
call me blessed;
for he who is mighty has done great things
for me,
and holy is his name (Luke 1:46-49).

After a three-month stay in the home of her kinswoman, she was ready to leave Judea and return to her own family. She must have wondered, many times along the way, about the experiences which lay ahead.

THE TOWN WHERE JOSEPH LIVED

"Her husband Joseph, being a just man and unwilling to put her to shame, resolved to divorce her quietly." Matt. 1:19

Mary's horizons were probably quite limited. She worked about her family's home. She was able to visit with neighbors at the well each day. When olives or figs or grapes were ripe, she joined the others to gather them. On the Sabbath she went to synagogue. But aside from feast days and weddings and burials and an occasional trip to Jerusalem, there was little variation in her daily life.

Joseph, on the other hand, could come and go from Nazareth at will. His little village probably adhered to strict Jewish customs, but famous roads like the Via Maris and other caravan routes ran nearby. Roman soldiers in flashing helmets and red capes traveled these roads. There were chariots, and rich people were carried on litters by their slaves. Camel caravans were a common sight. Often when he ran errands in other towns, Joseph would have met alien people and heard alien tongues.

No single word in Hebrew can be translated to mean "carpenter." But in the three languages used in Jesus' day, Aramaic, Greek, and Hebrew, there is a word meaning "cutters or workers in wood and stone and iron." Joseph was a worker in wood. For special jobs he may have used costly cedar, carried from Lebanon, or oak or sycamore. For everyday tasks he would have used olive wood, wild fig, and other woods he could find close to town. He would have gone out to the forested areas himself to fell a tree when he needed one. Probably, like others skilled in his trade, he knew how to treat sycamore to make it hard as iron to use for a plowshare.

Joseph would have helped prepare beams for roofs of many little houses around town, maneuvering them carefully through the crooked streets. He had no worktable. Instead, he learned how to hold a beam very skillfully between his feet while he worked on it.

It was the custom for people with a common trade to live together in a certain area of town. But Nazareth was too small to have

Left: Two-thousand-year-old olive trees in Jerusalem

many carpenters. Joseph's shop may have opened onto the street, with his living quarters located in the back.

His tools included an adz , bow drill, plane, hammer or mallet, knives, saw, hatchet, ax, and nails. Many nails were made of bronze.

A carpenter's shop in Nazareth

Right: Eastern dress, which in many particulars resembles the clothes of the first century: a cloak and a simple robe from neck to feet, with a girdle around the waist and fringes at the corners of the garment, in accordance with biblical injunction.

Bottom: Fringed garment

Besides heavier jobs such as mending rooftops or constructing new ones, Joseph would have done the work later assigned to woodcarvers and wheelwrights and cabinetmakers. Chairs were not used in the village homes, but stools were known. Joseph may have made the benches used in the local synagogue. He probably made the wooden chests in which clothing was stored, as well as the tripods used to hold lamps when they were not set in a wall niche.

Door lintels were of wood, and Joseph would have been asked, at times, to measure and cut these.

Quite possibly he did not earn a living solely from his trade. He may have had a field on the outskirts of town where he planted vegetables or grain. He would have owned a donkey to help him carry supplies from place to place, and he may also have had a goat or two for milk and cheese.

At this time the style of clothing had been greatly influenced by foreign taste. Ordinary people, both men and women, wore a linen undergarment or shirt. Over this Joseph would have worn a loose garment rather like Mary's, a tunic or coat. This was girdled or belted at the waist. A beautifully dyed or embroidered belt, which could be wound around the waist several times, was a symbol of status. Small items could be stored very handily in its folds.

Usually the coat was made of two pieces of cloth sewn together. Occasionally a person would have a coat woven in one piece without a seam. Jesus had such a coat at the time of the crucifixion and soldiers cast lots to see who would acquire it.

If Joseph adhered to the customs of orthodox Judaism, his coat would have been fringed at the bottom with ritual tassels. The ancient Jewish law gave careful instructions about this, including how the thread was to be twisted and how many knots were permitted. The tassels, often a deep shade of blue, signaled that the wearer was an upright Jew.

Whenever he was in a hurry or when he was working hard, Joseph could draw the hem of his tunic up between his legs and tuck it into his girdle where it would be out of the way. New Testament passages refer to this as "girding up one's loins."

Another garment, a cloak, was always a prized possession. It served many purposes. Heavy cloaks woven of camel hair were handed down from father to son. Joseph's cloak may have been of camel hair or wool. We can be certain it was warm and closely woven so it would be as waterproof as possible. Joseph used it

often as a blanket and as both bed and covering when he was away from home. Later, when Mary grew weary on the trip to Bethlehem, he may have folded his cloak to cushion her ride on the donkey's back.

The men of this time wore several styles of headdress. Sometimes, over a skullcap, a complicated turbanlike arrangement was worn, much like the turbans used in the Middle East today. Joseph may have worn the simpler, graceful piece of cloth tied around his head and draped over his shoulders to protect his neck from the sun as he worked. Like Mary, he would have owned sandals but he would have gone barefoot at times, too.

Ardent male Jews wore symbols in addition to tassels to show they were adhering to the Law. Joseph would have had two small square leather boxes, phylacteries, which he strapped onto his forehead and to his upper left arm when he was at prayer. These boxes contained tiny rolls of parchment tied with white hair from either a cow's or a calf's tail. The rolls were inscribed with special scriptural passages. Pharisees wore their phylacteries all the time and the fringes and tassels on their robes were very ornate. But Joseph was an artisan. To avoid defiling his phylacteries, he used them only when at prayer, along with a beautiful prayer shawl which covered his head and the upper portion of his body. Following ancient custom, he turned toward Jerusalem when he prayed.

On the Sabbath day he joined other men at the synagogue, taking his turn at various duties. The Law had to be read, not recited from memory, so unless Joseph knew how to read he would not have performed this job.

Phylacteries: Small leather boxes, strapped onto the forehead and upper left arm, while praying. They contain minute scrolls inscribed with biblical excerpts.

Right: Samaritan Torah, an ancient Pentateuch. Parchment Torahs were unrolled and read in the synagogue as a central part of religious service.

Each service began with the congregation facing Jerusalem to pray. One man — and it may have been Joseph sometimes — stood in front of the ark which held the sacred scrolls. He recited the ancient words of the *Shema* ("Hear, O Israel: the Lord our God is one Lord") and the *Shemoneh Esreh*, a collection of benedictions, while everyone else prayed in silence. The period of prayer ended with a resounding *Amen*.

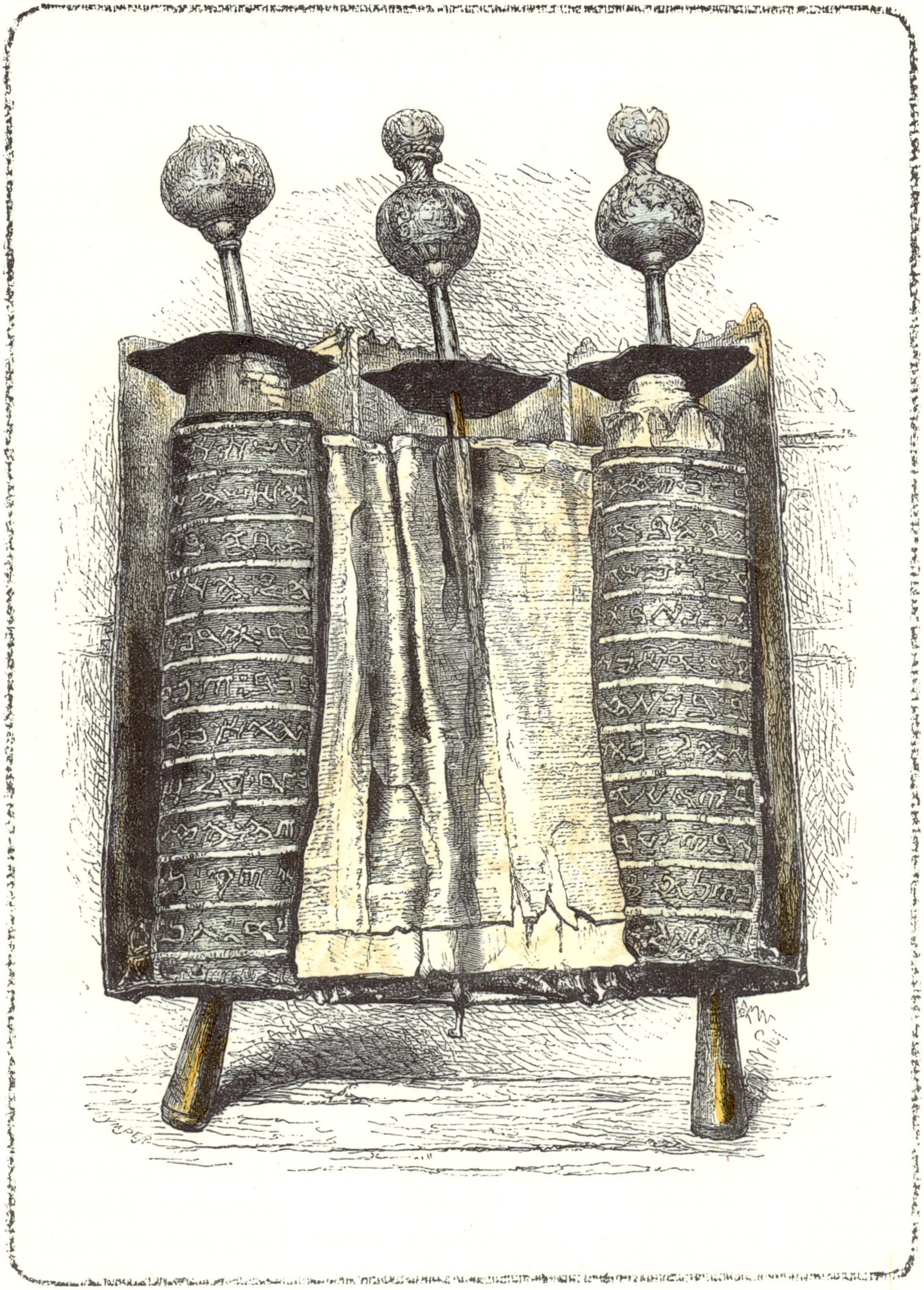

Throughout Nazareth and the surrounding area, Joseph had built a reputation as a just man. We do not know when Mary chose to share the news of the coming birth with him. Matthew tells us he was troubled and resolved to divorce her quietly so she would suffer no disgrace.

Perhaps he had climbed the steps to the rooftop of his house to sleep under the stars. And when he fell asleep, after mulling over the facts and reaching the difficult decision to divorce Mary, he dreamed that an angel of the Lord came to him. "Do not fear to make Mary your wife, for that which is conceived in her is of the Holy Spirit," said the angel.

What relief must have flooded through Joseph's mind and how many questions, too. He would have to visit Mary and her family soon and make arrangements to be married quietly without the usual seven days of merriment and feasting, dancing, and games. There would be none of the songs and riddles, probably no festal attire, no crowns for the bride and groom, no bridal canopy.

But perhaps Mary would be so happy to know he trusted her story now that she would not miss the gaiety of a traditional wedding celebration. Dressed in her finest garment, she would await Joseph's coming. Perhaps her mother would prepare a special meal that day, and later Joseph would take his bride home to live in his own dwelling. From that day forward she would be under his authority.

Would relatives and friends who expected an invitation to the wedding feast ask questions? Why had Joseph and Mary changed their minds? Memories of the dream, whirling inside of Joseph's head, gave him more important things to think about than the nagging questions of curious neighbors.

The angel had said that Mary's baby had been conceived of the Holy Spirit. What did this mean?

Right: Eastern wedding ceremonies

Overleaf: On the way to Bethlehem; the tomb of Rachel in foreground

For other men of Nazareth, life would continue in a quiet way. But for Joseph it would not be the same again.

THE WAY TO BETHLEHEM

"And Joseph also went up from Galilee, from the city of Nazareth, to Judea, to the city of David, which is called Bethlehem, because he was of the house and lineage of David, to be enrolled with Mary, his betrothed, who was with child." **Luke 2:4-5**

Joseph was from the town of Bethlehem. Shortly after Mary returned from Judea, he discovered he must go there himself, because Roman law required registration to pay certain taxes.

For Jews living under Roman rule, one of the bitterest blows was the conqueror's system of heavy taxation. All male Jews over 13 years of age were required by Jewish law to pay a half-shekel Temple tax. In addition, they paid the first-fruits tithe, a tenth of whatever the fields, gardens, and flocks produced each year. And now the extra burden of new Roman levies threatened to leave many Jews on the edge of poverty.

When possible, Caesar Augustus tried to keep conquered people content by letting them continue familiar customs. Local rulers, for instance, could remain in power if they paid tribute to Rome and promised to squelch any uprisings.

Herod had won favor this way. Some years after he had seized the entire land of Palestine unlawfully, the Romans had named him king of the Jews. In reality he was only another of the Romans' countless vassals.

The tax Joseph had to register for was an important one based on the amount and value of property a person owned. At first, the emperor had permitted Jewish elders to keep track of these statistics. But problems soon developed. Leery of Roman officials, the elders refused to give out accurate information. The emperor appointed an efficient Roman commission to get the job done properly.

Left: Roman soldiers

Coin from the first century B.C., the third year of Herod's reign. The legend reads: "To Herod the King."

Tradition pictures Mary and Joseph hurrying to Bethlehem and arriving the very night Jesus was born. Actually they must have realized in advance that it would be necessary to go.

Enrollment was a tedious affair. Joseph could not tell exactly when the registration committee would be in Bethlehem, the town of his ancestors. He simply had to guess and hope he might be right. Friends who had registered in other places may have let Joseph know the officials were working their way, little by little, through every town and village. Sometimes they spent as long as three months in one location.

Since this was a property tax, Joseph probably owned some family land, perhaps a vineyard, in the vicinity of Bethlehem. Otherwise he would have had no reason to make the journey.

If he wanted fair treatment from the Romans, there was no choice in the matter. Any Jew failing to appear in person at the right time might discover later, to his dismay, that his taxes were scandalously high.

The angel's reassuring appearance in a dream had been a sign to Joseph. Mary's story about the imminent birth was true. But it would be too risky to leave her to the mercy of neighbors, who would assume she had been unfaithful to him. So he persuaded her to make the trip southward again.

The Bible does not tell us when Mary and Joseph completed the betrothal agreement and became husband and wife. Translations of the Gospel of Luke mention that Joseph traveled to Bethlehem with his espoused wife. But Matthew describes how, immediately after his dream, Joseph rose and took Mary as his wife, although he "knew her not" until her baby was born.

As with Mary's previous journey, preparations for the trip must have been simple. Joseph probably looked for an uncle or brother or friend to take care of his shop during his absence. Or perhaps he decided to close the shop, leaving word with a neighbor that he would soon return. He did not suspect how long he would be gone!

Joseph, although not wealthy, probably owned a donkey to carry his carpenter's tools and supplies from place to place. Even the poorest families owned one of these dependable little creatures, so common on the dusty footpaths of Palestine.

Job and Isaiah mention the wild asses of the wilderness, animals that roamed the bare hillsides hunting for pasture and snorting into the wind. Domesticated donkeys were popular earlier than this. Strings of asses had long been carriers of freight in the Holy Land.

The family donkey, though obstinate, was a sturdy pack animal, surefooted on the stoniest paths leading over hills and steep ravines. Compared to a horse, a donkey required little barley for its daily ration.

Mary probably walked much of the way. Whenever she rode, she would sit sideways on the donkey's back. Quite possibly she took her spindle to use as she rode along. She would have packed a spare pair of sandals, and she and Joseph would have carried their heavy cloaks. The nights grew very chilly.

Donkey saddles, bells, and ornaments, as they were used from time immemorial, in vogue to this very day in villages in the area.

Other than a meager supply of food — a barley loaf or two, some dates, a fig cake, olives preserved in brine — there was little more to pack. They carried goatskin bags of water and possibly an empty gourd. There would be long distances between watering places and containers were not provided at the wells and springs. A traveler usually waited for a stranger to pass by with one in order to get a drink.

They would have traveled with a group of people or a caravan. At night they might have stopped near a caravanserai, or khan. If not, they might have slept on the ground, rolled in their cloaks with a stone for a pillow. Since Mary was pregnant, if they were near a settlement, strangers might have offered them lodging. The Jews prided themselves on being hospitable. Their law bade them to recall the days of their exile in a foreign land and to treat strangers with courtesy.

If the couple had set out in the fall before the heavy rains and had gone across the Plain of Jezreel, they would have seen farmers plowing and harrowing their fields of wheat and barley. Plows were crudely made of wood and iron and had no wheels. They had to be dragged across the land several times because they only

A wooden plow, illustrating how, in ancient times, oxen were yoked

scratched the earth and did not break it up. Sometimes asses or camels were harnessed to plows. More often, Mary and Joseph would have seen oxen doing the job. An old law said that two kinds of animals could not be yoked together.

The road across the plain was boggy in many places, and it joined the Jordan Valley road. Traveling in a large group, Mary and Joseph may have used this road. It is more likely that they chose to avoid the dangers and the steep ascent by following the central line of hills.

If it was fall, wherever there were vineyards they would have noticed grapes ripening on the vine. During the harvest, Mary and Joseph would have seen men and women and children wheeling fruit-laden carts to the winepress, or carrying heavy baskets of grapes.

Each vineyard had jackal scares made of small piles of whitewashed stones, and also a little watchtower. Often this was a wooden booth roofed over with leaves, but when they reached the

Grapes

Overleaf: Threshing corn

vineyards of Judea where wood was scarce, the watchtowers would have been of sun-dried brick or stone. The towers were set in a high place when possible, so members of a family might take turns on duty, ready to scare away wild animals or thieves at a moment's notice. Some families built a summer house in the middle of the vineyard for this purpose.

Hungry sojourners were permitted by law to eat their fill of grapes. They were not, however, allowed to fill vessels and carry away an additional supply of fruit.

The olive harvest came later, at the end of November, so Mary and Joseph were not likely to have been traveling at this time. The weather would have been too unpredictable.

If they set out, instead, as some scholars believe, when the winter rains were past, the grain would have been ripening on the plains and they would have been welcome to gather some of it as they passed. In fact, sheaves would have been piled in generous heaps at the corners of fields so widows or needy people or travelers such as Mary and Joseph might help themselves without asking.

In spring a traveler passing through lower Galilee would notice the pink blossoms of the flax everywhere, as well as anemone and many other flowers. The leaves of the gnarled old olive trees shimmered blue-green in the sunlight.

When they grew tired, Mary and Joseph may have rested beneath the umbrellalike shade of the fig tree. No matter if it happened to be near someone's dwelling. The Scriptures said, "When a stranger sojourns with you in your land, you shall not do him wrong. The stranger who sojourns with you shall be to you as the native among you, and you shall love him as yourself; for you were strangers in the land of Egypt" (Lev. 19:33-34).

Mary and Joseph would not have expected to find this hospitality in Samaria because Jews from Galilee and Judea considered the mixed peoples who had settled there heretics. Samaritans believed only in the Pentateuch, the first five books of the Old Testament.

They worshiped not at Jerusalem, but at a temple on Mt. Gerizim. But this part of Palestine had been the scene of famous battles in the old days, and the home of many Jewish heroes. Possibly, as they traversed Samaria, Mary and Joseph recalled the stories of Elijah and Elisha, and some of the warnings of the Judean herdsman, Amos, concerning the extravagant and decadent life of the people who had lived here.

Herod had rebuilt the capital city, Samaria, in Hellenistic style, with a temple honoring Caesar, and had given it a new Greek name, Sebaste.

By the second evening, on the ridge road, the couple might have reached Judea. Across the border, they would have found water and shelter at a caravanserai in existence since ancient times. The following day they might have proceeded to Bethel, the spot where Abraham had pitched his tent and where he had built an altar. Here too Jacob had dreamed of angels, constructing a stone pillar as his pledge to God.

Samaria, from the Holy Mountain, Gerizim

Naturally they would wish to get settled in Bethlehem without delay so Joseph could be about his business. The jolting ride on the donkey's back must have made Mary realize that her baby would be arriving soon. If they were traveling close to Jerusalem in a festal season, especially at Passover, they might have stopped to pay a visit to the Temple. Otherwise, they would have skirted the city.

Less than two miles from the Holy City, when the walls and towers came into sudden view, most travelers stopped to drink in the sight. From this point, Mary and Joseph saw the Upper City with its residential dwellings on the high western hill, and the valley that cut through the heart of the city. They could see the bridge leading across this valley to the Temple in the Lower City.

In the right-hand corner of the north wall of Jerusalem gleamed the citadel Herod the Great had built to honor Mark Antony. Travelers on this road would notice the Roman soldiers keeping guard from the towers of the citadel overlooking the courts of the Temple.

In the northeastern corner of the Upper City they would spot another landmark, Herod's sumptuous palace.

Jerusalem and Bethlehem were separated by undulating hills. At one point along the way, both towns were clearly visible. The tiny limestone dwellings of Bethlehem, blending into the surrounding buff-colored rocky hills, were a dramatic contrast to the grandeur of Jerusalem.

Mary and Joseph had traveled three full days, perhaps four. There had been no way to hurry the plodding donkey. Mary must have been relieved to see, at last, the terraced hillsides and the little homes of Bethlehem. Deep in her heart, she hoped it would not take long to find a place to stay that night. Her baby would be born soon, soon!

Right: Mount Zion, from the Hill of the Evil Counsel

Overleaf: Bethlehem

THE CHRISTMAS CITY

"And while they were there, the time came for her to be delivered. And she gave birth to her firstborn son and wrapped him in swaddling cloths, and laid him in a manger, because there was no place for them in the inn." Luke 2:6-7

In the old days, Bethlehem had been known as Ephrathah or Ephrath. *Bet Lechem* means "house of bread," an appropriate name for this tiny settlement in one of the few fertile spots of Judea. The town is perched on the summit of a limestone spur, about five miles south of the Holy City.

Long ago another couple had journeyed this way from Bethel. It was near Bethlehem that Jacob's wife Rachel had died during childbirth, leaving him his youngest son, Benjamin. And Jacob had marked the spot where she was buried with a stone pillar.

In Bethlehem, Ruth the Moabite had settled with her mother-in-law at the beginning of the barley harvest. Consumed with homesickness, she had looked out over the wadis and hills and desert, longing for her native land of Moab.

Here Samuel anointed David, the youngest son of Jesse, with holy oil, preparing him to be king. Later, during a famous harvest season when the Philistines were garrisoned within, David thirsted for water from "the well by the gate," actually a rock-carved cistern. When three of his men risked their lives to get it for him, he poured the water out on the ground as a libation to the Lord, deeming it too precious to drink.

When Mary and Joseph came to Bethlehem, in addition to the cisterns there were reservoirs called Solomon's Pools a few miles south on the road to Hebron. But these supplied water to Jerusalem, not Bethlehem.

The road from Jerusalem to Hebron was important. Caravaners traveling it often stopped at the caravanserai outside the gate of Bethlehem for food and water and shelter.

Left: Rachel's tomb near Bethlehem with terraced hills in background

Overleaf: Roman masonry in Jerusalem

The caravanserai or khan was not a real inn in any modern sense of the word. Quite possibly it was little more than an open space surrounded by a wall and a colonnade. Beneath the arches of the colonnade were small rooms for travelers. Often the animals were not stabled but simply gathered in the center of the khan. When a khan had some sort of stable, it was usually a limestone cave.

There was seldom a host. If the khan happened to be overcrowded, a weary traveler would spend the night in a corner of the courtyard, or in an enclosed place among the cattle, or in the cavelike stable if one existed.

Mary and Joseph may have stayed in such a place. The Greek word *katalyma,* used in the Gospel of Luke, does not mean "inn." It implies shelter for man and beast where burdens are removed. Or Joseph may have expected to rent or borrow the upper room on the roof of someone's dwelling, the place reserved for a sojourner or guest.

If the little town was crowded with pilgrims and other travelers and no room was available, Mary and Joseph might have been offered the use of one of the cave-stables so common to the houses built against the hillsides. Joseph would have been able to convert any small corner into comfortable living quarters.

In any case, mothers had long found an empty manger an excellent cradle for a baby. In decent weather the cattle would be out on the hillside grazing. It was natural for Mary to think of using a manger for baby Jesus. It was much safer than rolling him in a blanket and setting him on the platform in the house or khan where he easily might be pushed off by mistake. Perhaps Joseph covered the prickly straw with his cloak or a blanket to make a soft bed for his newborn son.

Frequently a midwife attended the birth of a baby, but the Bible does not mention the presence of any such person. We may surmise that Mary, being a flesh and blood person, felt the pains of labor as much as any woman giving birth to her child.

According to the custom, someone — in this case probably Joseph — would have rubbed the body of baby Jesus with salt. It was believed that this would "harden" the flesh and make the infant strong. Jesus would have been oiled carefully, too, with olive oil, and then wrapped tightly in many yards of cloth before he was set gently into the empty manger. Birth was a common event and there does not seem to have been much fuss over the birth of Jesus.

Close by the manger, Mary and Joseph looked down on the baby, knowing something wonderful had happened. Out on a Judean hillside, in the fields near Bethlehem, a group of awestruck shepherds were visited by the heavenly host who brought them tidings of great joy!

A typical peasants' home, with manger. The family occupies the raised dais. The steps over the arch lead to the grain storage area. Dried fruits hang from the rafters.

Overleaf: Olive trees in the fields of Bethlehem

THE FIELDS
NEAR BETHLEHEM

"And in that region there were shepherds out in the field, keeping watch over their flock by night. And an angel of the Lord appeared to them, and the glory of the Lord shone around them, and they were filled with fear. And the angel said to them, 'Be not afraid; for behold, I bring you good news of a great joy which will come to all the people; for to you is born this day in the city of David a Savior, who is Christ the Lord.'" Luke 2:8-11

In early times the first people who moved into the Holy Land were shepherds looking for water and pastures for their flocks. There are many Old Testament stories about shepherds. We read of Abraham and Lot arguing over pasture lands, and of David staying at home to tend his father's sheep while his brothers fought the Philistines. The prophets tell of the shepherd's life, and the psalmist sings of it. But the most cherished story is the one Luke relates about the shepherds who were visited by a heavenly host in the field near Bethlehem at the time of the holy birth.

In the time of Jesus there were two kinds of shepherds in Palestine. Some were true nomads. Others, although wandering over plateaus and hills seeking pasture for their flocks to graze, were not. The nomadic shepherds lived in tents woven from goat hair. For centuries men and women wove cloth for the family's tent in narrow strips on a handloom. Eventually guilds of weavers were organized to make the many varieties of cloth which merchants then sold in the marketplace. But the handloom continued to be used and certainly most shepherd nomads would have done their own weaving.

Because the goat hair ranged from black to brownish-black, a new tent was a very dark color until the blazing sun bleached it to a golden, toasty shade. Each year a shepherd, or more probably his wife or daughters, mended any torn places with fresh strips of cloth. Sewn alongside the old faded pieces, the new strips gave the tent a peculiar striped appearance.

Left: In the shepherds' field, Bethlehem. A shepherd watering a flock of the longeared and longtailed sheep common in the Holy Land

Rain made the goatskin tent stretch taut until it became quite waterproof. At times the desert shepherds moved about, taking their families with them. Often they left their families at the tent site and went off alone with their flock to seek better pasture.

Many shepherds lived a rough existence, but the nomad was especially isolated. For days on end, he saw no other person. Sometimes, when he ran across another shepherd, the two grazed their flocks together for a while, taking turns at night so one could sleep while the other watched for wolves and other wild beasts.

At sundown the sheep were gathered into a fold roughly constructed of vines and stones piled in a wall. Sometimes several flocks were sheltered in the same fold. Every one of the sheep recognized its own name and knew the special guttural call of its master, so it was not difficult for a shepherd to gather his flock together when the pink light of dawn crept over the hills.

If a lamb or an old ewe was missing, he hunted the ravines for it, carrying it home across his shoulder if he discovered it had been injured or when it was too tired to walk. He knew how to anoint an animal's wounds with the oil he stored in an empty ram's horn. If a shepherd was alone at night, he lay down across the doorway of the fold to protect his flock from harm.

Tents of a small camp

Right: Shepherds gathering their flock into caves in the cliffs of the Kidron Valley

WHYMPER

Desert flocks remained out in the open through the year. Snow fell primarily in the hill country of northern Palestine. During years when snow fell in the vicinity of Jerusalem and Hebron it seldom remained on the ground very long. But the winter days were raw and cold and dreary. During the worst weather, a shepherd might shelter his flock in one of the natural limestone caves in the hills. In one of these very caves, a modern Bedouin came upon the famous Dead Sea Scrolls.

The most common sheep of Palestine was the broadtailed sheep. Sometimes the tail of this creature weighed as much as 15 pounds. It was a most useful source of food fat. In addition to providing meat and milk and fat, the sheep was also valued for its wool, which could be sheared and woven into clothing. The entire sheepskin was used by the shepherd too. He fashioned it into a cloak after tanning it with the wool left on it.

Some of the sheep were of a horned variety. Their horns could be used to store oil. Since earliest times, a ram's horn had been heated and fashioned into a special musical instrument. Heating made it possible to flatten the horn and to turn the end of it up. It was used on many occasions in the old days to sound alarms and to announce the accession of a king to the throne. The Temple ram's horn or *shofar* called the people to worship on great feast days.

The broadtailed sheep, whose horns were used to make musical instruments

By the time Jesus was born, many shepherds wore an under-tunic. Their outer cloak might have been sheepskin, but frequently it was woven wool in wide gray and black stripes. Called a *simlah,* it sheltered the wearer from sun and rain and from the winter snows. The shepherd's girdle was of cloth or leather. In its pockets he carried coins and other small items such as pebbles. These he tossed when he needed to get the sheep's attention.

Beneath his cloak a shepherd wore a very crude homespun robe. A loop of twisted goat's hair held his napkinlike headdress securely over his long hair.

The ram's horn or *shofar* still sounds in synagogues on great feasts.

The shepherd carried a staff or crook. Its curved end proved invaluable whenever he needed to rescue a sheep marooned on a rocky ledge. He was seldom without a heavy club and a sling similar to the one David had used centuries earlier. His goatskin bag held water and also made a good churn for butter and for the special thick kind of yogurt made of milk which had been partly evaporated and then fermented. This dish, *leban,* is still relished today in many Mideastern countries.

Devout Jews were scornful of desert shepherds. They looked on them as "wild men" or scoundrels, half-crazy nomads, because they were unkempt and their hard work prevented them from keeping the sacred feasts or attending services in the Temple. Their rough life-style did not permit them to obey the ancient dietary laws, either. Many times they were suspected of thievery.

The shepherds who did not lead a nomadic existence took their sheep out to the hills to graze but returned to a stable or cave in one of the little villages at night. During the months when no rain fell, they went farther afield, sleeping beneath the vast canopy of stars with their flocks safely sheltered in a makeshift fold.

Perhaps the shepherds in the Christmas story were nomads. But near Bethlehem were the fields where the sheep intended for Temple sacrifice were kept. The shepherds tending these flocks may well have been the ones who heard the singing of the angels and hurried to the manger.

Right: Typical shepherd's dress

Overleaf: Mount Moriah, Jerusalem's Temple Mount, first century

The shepherds remain forever anonymous. But Luke tells us that they shared with others the wonderful experience they had that night. And they returned to the fields whence they had come, glorifying and praising God!

THE TEMPLE

"And when the time came for their purification according to the law of Moses, they brought him up to Jerusalem to present him to the Lord." **Luke 2:22**

Two important rituals were required after the birth of Jesus. The first was circumcision. People of many cultures were accustomed to circumcising, but for the Jews the operation took on profound spiritual meaning. From the days when Abraham had made his covenant with God, this outer physical sign marked the day the son became a true member of the Holy Nation. The Old Testament as well as the New speaks of inner circumcision of the heart.

At the time a baby boy was circumcised, he received his name. In most cases the father selected it. This time the angel had already chosen it. The name Jesus is probably based on the Hebrew *Yeshua* or savior, which occurs many times in the Old Testament. The rite of circumcision took place when the baby was eight days old. Jews believed it to be so necessary that it was one of the few acts which could be performed on a Sabbath if the Sabbath happened to be the eighth day after the birth.

The second ritual was the purification of the mother. Like most other ancient peoples, Jews were awed by blood. They sensed a terrifying mystery about it. It was believed to be the seat of the life force, and Jews were afraid of its polluting power.

For 40 days after the birth of her boy baby, Mary was thought to be unclean. Had her infant turned out to be a girl, the period would have been doubled. Until undergoing the ritual of purification, Mary was disqualified from any participation in worship. She was not permitted to enter the sanctuary, nor was she allowed to touch any hallowed item. It was customary for a woman to remain confined inside her house at this time.

The sacrifice for her purification could be offered by proxy. However, like any faithful Jewish couple who lived close enough to the Temple, Mary and Joseph wished to go there in person.

Left: A humble offering of turtledoves, the sacrifice of the poor

Mary and Joseph probably walked from Bethlehem to the Holy City. They would have seen traders and merchants, wealthy people riding on camels or in litters carried by slaves, Roman soldiers on horseback, tax collectors, foreigners, and pilgrims.

To the pagan traveler, Jerusalem was merely another city. To Jews it was a holy place, one they loved from the depths of their very being. No matter in what distant land they lived, the one thing all Jews longed to do was to make a pilgrimage to the Holy City.

"If I forget you, O Jerusalem," cried out the psalmist, "let my right hand wither" (Ps. 137:5).

The Golden Gate, Jerusalem

As they climbed the steep hill approaching the gates of the city, with the Temple in sight at last, pilgrims burst into happy songs. Mary and Joseph, radiant over the birth of their baby and journeying there on an important mission, may have joined in one of these songs of ascent.

I was glad when they said to me,
"Let us go to the house of the Lord!"
Our feet have been standing
within your gates, O Jerusalem! (Ps. 122:1-2).

For the Lord has chosen Zion;
he has desired it for his habitation:
"This is my resting place forever;
here will I dwell, for I have desired it" (Ps. 132:13-14).

From a distance, the native yellow limestone walls and towers of the city made it look golden against the cloudless Judean sky. The Valley of Hinnom bordered Jerusalem on the west and the Valley of Kidron on the east. East of the city and the Valley of Kidron was the Mount of Olives, a ridge slightly higher than Jerusalem. Beyond the Mount of Olives, the terrain made an abrupt descent to nearly 1300 feet below sea level. The rolling hilly region continued northward. To the south was a continuation of the ridge on which Jerusalem was located.

Jerusalem was no longer the proud and glorious capital it had been during the reign of King David, yet it was a cosmopolitan city. Foreigners conversed in strange tongues. Mary and Joseph saw Ethiopians, Egyptians, Romans, Greeks, Arabians, Persians, Jews in Hellenized dress, as well as more conservative Jews wearing fringed robes and phylacteries.

Outside the massive walls, near the Pool of Siloam, fullers would have been processing cloth, and at the Fish Gate dealers hawked their dried fish. So narrow were the streets of the Holy City that wheeled vehicles were forbidden inside the gates. It was difficult enough for a donkey laden with goods or a Roman soldier on horseback to maneuver up and down the stone steps leading from one street level to the next. By modern standards the streets were short and very crooked.

To Mary, a peasant girl used to the quiet village ways of Nazareth, Jerusalem would have seemed a fascinating place, full of tantalizing sounds and sights and smells. There were two main streets, the Upper Market and the Lower Market, where a person could purchase dried figs, spices and perfumes from distant Arabia, cheese, cloth, and dates, beautiful jewelry and exotic products from mysterious, far-off places.

Craftsmen congregated in shops along the streets devoted to their particular wares, the weavers on one street, the perfumers on another, the bakers on still another. Behind each shop was the small working area used by its owner.

At this time a valley intersected the city, separating its two main hills. It has been identified by scholars as the Tyropoean Valley, the Valley of the Cheesemakers, mentioned by Josephus. Through the years it has become filled with rubbish and now it is little more than a slight depression in the ground.

King Herod, enthralled with the beauty of the Hellenistic culture, had used classical architecture everywhere, except in designing the new Temple he was building for the Jews. Among the public buildings he had erected were an amphitheater outside the city gates and a theater within, a hippodrome, a palace, and the Antonia Fortress, conveniently overlooking the Temple so Roman soldiers could prevent serious uprisings.

The houses of the Upper City were large, with beautiful gardens. Each house had its own cistern. Both the city's aqueducts drew water from three reservoirs to the south. The water in the Upper Aqueduct was piped to the magnificent gardens surrounding Herod's sumptuous palace. The Lower Aqueduct supplied much of the water needed in the Temple after the daily sacrifices.

Every one of the enormous gates of the city was fortified and each had a name: Fish Gate, Fountain Gate, Gate of Ephraim, Dung Gate. On the east, the Golden Gate led directly to the Temple, but the main access was on the southern side. Thus the public entered Jerusalem through Hulda's Gates (often called the Double Gate and the Triple Gate) in the southern wall. A wide flight of stone steps led from the street along the foot of the wall down to a plaza. In the middle of the plaza was a building used for ritual baths. On this level, too, were rows of shops for the benefit of the crowds of worshipers and pilgrims who strolled there.

Several centuries before (587 B.C.) the armies of Nebuchadnezzar had destroyed the Temple built by Solomon. Later Zerubbabel had erected another. And now Herod was determined to replace it with a magnificent edifice larger and more splendid than any building the Jews had seen before. Aware of their sullen hatred, he hoped to placate them and gain new respect. He ordered tons of material to be carried in for fill, to level the ground so that Mt. Moriah could be transformed into a mammoth rectangular platform.

Many Jews felt certain that the king would destroy their sacred Temple and then refuse to replace it. To allay their fears, Herod hit upon the ingenious idea of tearing down only one portion at a time and rebuilding it before he proceeded further. It took only 18 months to complete the sanctuary proper, but work on the entire complex of buildings and courtyards was to continue for more than 40 years. Herod would not live to see the finished Temple, so ornamented with gold that it was dazzling in the sun. His fantastic building enterprise was to exist for only a few decades before it would be destroyed forever.

Many thousands of men did the work. Some say 10,000; others estimate nearly 18,000. Herod had seen to it that 1000 priests especially trained as stone masons were the only ones designated to work on the most sacred parts of the Temple.

When they went through the gates, Mary and Joseph found themselves in the spacious Court of the Gentiles. Anyone was permitted to stroll here, even the heretic, the ritually unclean, the unbeliever. A few rules did apply. Nobody could carry a stick here. And it was not permissible to spit on the ground!

During the day this big rectangular area was as busy and as noisy as a Roman forum. Among the throngs, Mary and Joseph would have seen small groups of people standing around gossiping or discussing business affairs. Perhaps they noticed someone napping in the early morning sun. Here and there clusters of learned Jews, doctors of the law, might be arguing. Money changers exchanged the pagan coins of pilgrims for money that would be ritually clean. In the Court of the Gentiles Mary arranged for her own offering, either two turtledoves or two young pigeons, since that was what Mosaic law specified for one too poor to afford a yearling lamb.

Adjacent to the court, along three sides of the Temple platform, ran a flat-roofed portico with two rows of Corinthian columns.

The portico on the east side was known as Solomon's Porch. From here one could see the Mount of Olives and the Valley of Kidron.

It was probably in the outer court that Simeon, an elderly and devout man of prayer, was moved to take the baby in his arms and murmur those famous words of praise so often sung in churches today:

> *"Lord, now lettest thou thy servant depart in peace,*
> *according to thy word;*
> *for mine eyes have seen thy salvation*
> *which thou hast prepared in the presence of*
> *all peoples,*
> *a light for revelation to the Gentiles,*
> *and for glory to thy people Israel"* (Luke 2:29-32).

Inspired by the Spirit, Simeon recognized that Jesus was destined to play a special role in the history of Israel. The Gospel of Luke relates how Mary and Joseph marveled at the old man's words. Simeon must have especially touched young Mary's heart, for he went on to speak of the pain she would feel in coming years when her son became a leader.

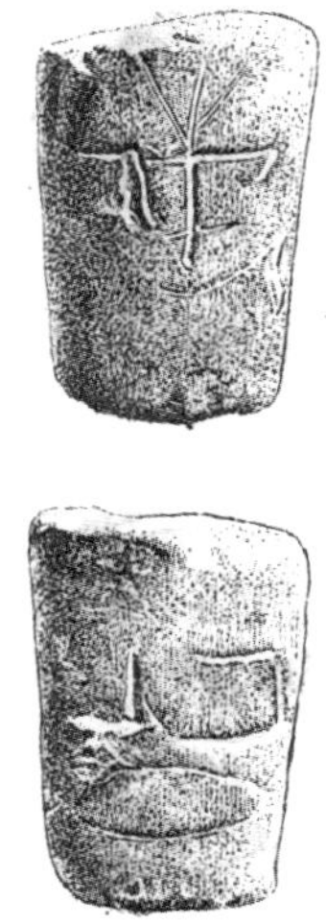

A recent discovery from the first century temple. The Hebrew inscription on the stone vessel, in which offerings were made, reads: "Korban" — sacrifice.

Among the crowds mingling there they met, too, the inspired old prophetess Anna who fasted and prayed daily at the Temple. Nobody lived at the Temple, yet the Bible implies that some arrangement had been made so the 84-year-old prophetess could remain continuously in the vicinity. Like Simeon, she offered thanks to God and spoke in a mysterious manner of the redemption long awaited by pious Jews.

Each part of the Temple was higher than the previous area. A visitor gained the impression of ascending steadily toward Almighty God. Bearing their offering, Mary and Joseph climbed the steps leading to the outer wall of the sanctuary. Signs were posted to inform non-Jews that they must go no farther. The penalty would be death.

The Temple building towered above the next restricted courts that surrounded it. Each level was connected by staircases.

First was the spacious Court of Women. Any Jew could enter here, but women could not go beyond this point. There were offering boxes, constructed with narrow necks to prevent dishonest people from helping themselves to coins. In each corner of the court was a chamber, one for the use of Nazirites, one for lepers, one for the storage of wood, and a fourth where oil was kept.

The next court, the Court of the Israelites, was open to male Jews who need not be priest or Levite. It seems to have had several entrances, the most noteworthy being the semicircular flight of steps with the Nicanor Gate. An Alexandrian Jew had presented this magnificently ornamented gate. It is said that it was so heavy that it took 20 strong men to open it each day. The rumbling of its opening signaled that the early morning sacrifice would soon begin.

Here, in the colonnade, the Sanhedrin met in a chamber of hewn stone. Compared to the Court of Women, the Court of Israelites was long and narrow and quite small. On festal occasions it became very crowded.

From this court, three more steps behind a balustrade led to the sacred Court of the Priests. There were in the Holy Land at this time thousands of priests and thousands of the priest-assistants known as Levites who did more menial tasks. All of them were assigned a week of duty at the Temple during the span of a year.

There was one high priest. He alone wore the special knee-length ephod or breastplate garment. The fabric of his ephod was dyed in sacred colors — scarlet, blue, and purple — woven through and through with shining golden threads. A semiprecious stone fastened to each shoulder contained six of the names of the 12 tribes of Israel. The front of the ephod was decorated with a jeweled breastplate and on it was a pocket containing the sacred parchment. The high priest wore a girdle, and a mitre on his head. From the hem of his ephod hung 72 small golden bells. Between them were embroidered pomegranate flowers, shining blue and purple and scarlet.

The high priest had many special rights because of his important office. No one else could enter the Holy of Holies to stand in the presence of God, and the high priest himself only entered there once a year, on the Day of Atonement.

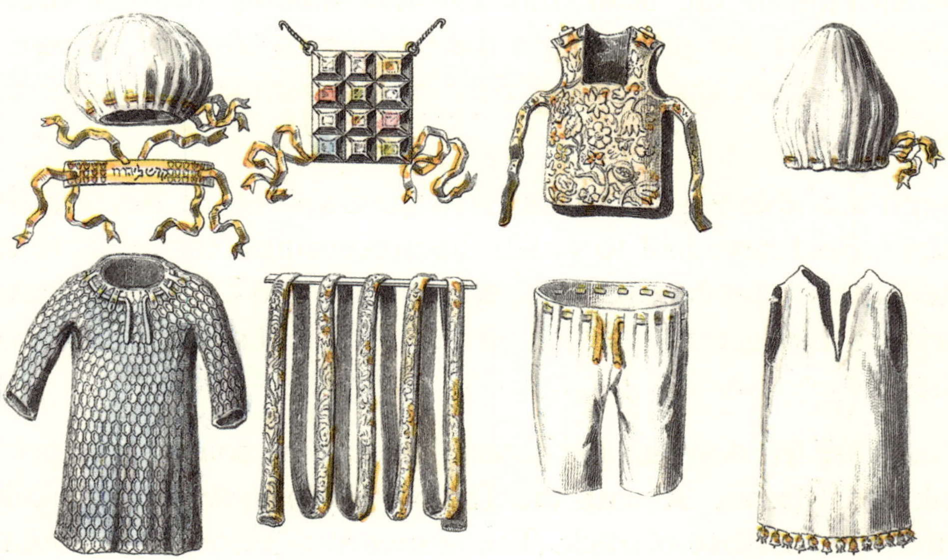

The vestments of the high priest

The Court of Priests covered a large area. On the northern and southern ends could be found halls used for various purposes. One was a stable for animals about to be sacrificed. Here, in front of the main part of the Temple, was the enormous altar of burnt offerings, an unhewn block of stone said to be 48 feet high. To one side were the marble tables where animals were slaughtered, since only pigeons were killed on the altar. On the other side was the large laver basin used for ritual washings.

The entrails of the dead animals were thrown into the fire. It probably was not possible for the heavy rich smell of incense to mask completely the stench of fresh blood, burning fat, and animal flesh.

Joseph was able to go on through to the Court of the Israelites, but Mary would have had to watch the proceedings from afar. Priests entered this court by five gates, each named and used for a definite purpose: the gates of flame, offerings, kindling, firstlings, and water.

A staircase led down to the cistern beneath the court where priests took ritual baths. Beneath the Temple platform were many other cisterns carved out of rock. The system was extremely elaborate.

A priest and the high priest

The largest cistern, often called the Great Sea, could hold an enormous supply of water. Aqueducts carried the water to cisterns. Steps led from the Court of Priests to the Temple. Above its porch Herod had dared to hang a wretched pagan symbol, the golden eagle of Rome. Furious Jews later tore it down in a riot when they believed Herod was dead. They paid with their lives, since the king was living after all.

A vestibule projected on either side of the eastern end of the Holy Place, making the ground plan of the entire Temple T-shaped. The priest entered the vestibule through an opening surrounded by columns. The cedar door of the sanctuary was covered with gold. Suspended over the doorway was a golden vine of grape clusters and leaves. Around the Holy Place was a gallery paneled with cedar and cypress. Here were three stories of offices and rooms.

The Holy Place contained the table for the showbread and the majestic seven-branched *menorah* or candlestick, as well as the small gold-covered altar where incense was burned at dawn and in the evening each day.

Temple vessels (from left to right): incense spoon, candelabrum, table for showbread, and trumpets, taken as booty to Rome after the destruction of the Temple in A.D. 70. Scene carved in relief on the Arch of Titus, Rome.

The entrance to the Holy of Holies was on the far wall. There was not a single thing there except bare rock. It was the dwelling place of the God of Israel.

One of the birds offered by Mary was burned completely as a sacrifice. Only the fat of the other was burned. The flesh of it belonged to the priests.

Long ago, God had commanded the Israelites to give him their firstborn animals and sons. Like other men, Joseph wanted "to buy his son back," so, before leaving the Temple, he paid the customary redemption price. Five shekels seemed a large sum to a "worker in wood," but it would relieve the baby of the priestly duties he would otherwise be required to perform later on.

Before returning to Bethlehem, the couple may have rested beneath the shade of a tree so Mary could suckle her baby while Joseph found some dates or figs for them to munch along the way. Perhaps they took time to wander through the market. Joseph may even have brought with him a small wooden item made with his own hands, to trade for a gift for his wife, who once again was ritually clean. Perhaps he bargained for a bracelet or a new ring, and a rattle for the baby.

Then they set out once again, with the strange words of old Simeon ringing in their ears: "Lord, now lettest thou thy servant depart in peace...for mine eyes have seen thy salvation."

Holding her infant son close, Mary may have buried the words in her heart, where they could not trouble her for the time being. How happy she would be to go home to Galilee! How eager she must have been to show her baby to relatives and friends in her own town!

Overleaf: Pyramids of Giza

The Temple of Herod the Great seen from a southeastern angle. Reconstruction by Melchior Comte de Vogüé, 1864

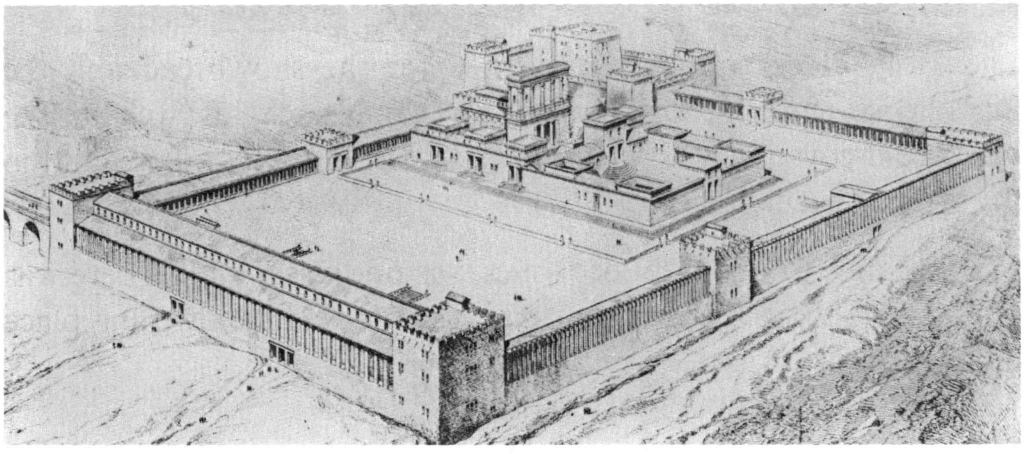

THE LAND OF EGYPT

"Behold, an angel of the Lord appeared to Joseph in a dream and said, 'Rise, take the child and his mother, and flee to Egypt.' " **Matt. 2:13**

While Mary and Joseph were living in a home in Bethlehem, probably in one of the upper rooms reserved for guests, the Wise Men appeared from a distant country. Persia? Chaldea? Nobody knows. Versed in the ancient science of astrology, they had noticed a new star and followed it to Bethlehem, supposing it to herald the birth of an important world leader.

At Jerusalem they stopped to ask directions from King Herod. The king, half-crazy and violently suspicious of anyone who might rob him of his throne, was disturbed enough to gather the chief priests and scribes and other important leaders to discuss the troubling question — exactly where was this child to be born?

He was informed that the prophets had written that a ruler would one day come from Bethlehem. Herod summoned the strangers privately. After questioning them further about the star, he bade them let him know as soon as they found the child, intimating that he, too, would like to pay a royal visit to worship the baby.

According to the spare, beautiful words of Matthew, "When they had heard the king they went their way; and lo, the star which they had seen in the East went before them, till it came to rest over the place where the child was" (2:9).

Rejoicing, the Wise Men entered the house and bowed down and worshiped the baby. They opened their treasures before him — gold, frankincense, and myrrh.

They seemed to be familiar with the caravan routes. After being warned in a dream not to return to Herod, they "departed to their own country by another way."

After their departure, Joseph, too, had a dream. An angel told him to flee with his family to Egypt. Herod's jealous rages were well

Left: Water buffalo being watered on the Nile, a common sight in Egypt for the past 6000 years

known to the Jews, who feared him and hated him. Had he not recently killed several members of his immediate family? No telling what he might do next!

Mary and Joseph, being forewarned, may have vanished from Bethlehem before the news spread abroad of the king's evil plan to murder every male baby under two years of age. Later they would shudder, perhaps have terrible nightmares, whenever they recalled their narrow escape. Surely tears would spring to Mary's eyes when the male babies of her friends near Bethlehem came to mind.

Following the exciting visit of the stately strangers from a far country and their generous gifts, this terrible warning of Herod's plan would have been hard to fathom. Mary and Joseph must have longed to send a swift, secret message to relatives and to a few close friends. How would loved ones in Nazareth know they were safely on the way to Egypt?

For hundreds of years, Egypt had enjoyed the reputation of being a prosperous country. There were famine years, of course, but most of the time Egypt was able to supply grain to many other countries. In the early days, Hebrew nomads had made the long trek down into Egypt. We read of Jacob's sons going there, and of Joseph becoming a ruler under one of the Pharaohs. The Hebrews' sojourn in that country was to last for many years. During some periods, notably during the lifetime of Moses, they were oppressed there. At other times, they had such a prosperous, contented existence that thousands of them decided to settle permanently.

Legends portray Mary and Joseph and their baby hastening off to Egypt by themselves. But nobody would dream of traversing those vast desert wastes alone! Bethlehem was close to a caravan route. The caravans set off about two or three o'clock in the morning to avoid the sweltering heat of the midday sun. It is likely that the couple arose hours before dawn to join one of these groups.

The camels used for caravan travel were capable of carrying extremely heavy burdens, often six or eight hundred pounds. They covered great distances without food or water. Most important for the holy family's flight was the speed with which the camels' padded feet were able to manage the desert sands.

In a caravan there was a place for a mother and her infant to ride, perhaps in a kind of palanquin. The beast's owner often rode either in the baggage saddle when it was empty, or on top of the load if it was not.

Quite possibly Mary and Joseph made their way south to that ancient city of refuge, Hebron. Perched on a slope in a valley high above sea level, Hebron was famous for its grapes and its beautiful olive groves. Long ago Abraham had buried his wife, Sarah, in a nearby cave. And here David had reigned over Judah for more than seven years, until he captured Jerusalem and it became the capital city.

If Mary and Joseph traveled this way, what pain they must have felt, gazing on beloved landmarks and wondering how long it might be before they set eyes on them again.

A halt in the desert — still a long way for the caravan to travel

The great hall of columns in the Temple of Karnak

Right: Red granite obelisk of Heliopolis, a greater part of its base now covered by the accumulated silt of time

Less than 30 miles away, on the edge of the wasteland, was Beersheba, a source of abundant water for the thirsty flocks of Abraham and Jacob. Near this place, Mary and Joseph's caravan group may have joined other caravans for the sake of safety, before picking up the route along the Mediterranean shore which had long joined Palestine to Egypt.

Close to the Nile delta they started the most difficult part of their journey over the sandy desert. Lagoons hidden here and there beneath the sand often fooled travelers into thinking they were on solid ground. It was hard to predict the shifting of the desert sands. Many days would have passed before the couple found relief from the exhausting heat, the metallic brightness of the sun, the surrounding, all-engulfing sea of sand. Mary and Joseph may have spoken at times of Moses' years of wandering with his people. Even if Jesus rode in his mother's arms in an enclosed place on a camel's back, he would have been exposed to the gritty sand blowing in the wind.

Water was scarce and their diminishing supply could not be replenished. How did Mary attend to her baby's needs? How did she continue to have milk to nurse him in such trying circumstances? How did she and Joseph manage to carry out the Mosaic laws concerning the ritual washing of their hands before they ate a meal?

As soon as they reached Rhinocolura they were across the border and safe from Herod's jurisdiction. Probably the holy family did not linger at the next city, Pelusium, although they would have wished to end their arduous journey as soon as possible. The swampy northeast corner of the delta seemed to encourage epidemics of the plague. Old Testament books refer to "the evil diseases of Egypt" and also to the destruction of entire armies by the pestilence.

In trying to quench her thirst from one of the brackish wells, Mary may have recalled the refreshing water of the well at Nazareth and longed for home.

The scattering of Jews throughout various countries is called the Diaspora or the Dispersion. When Jesus was born, thousands of Jews were living outside Palestine. In Egypt alone, according to the writings of Philo, a million Jews had settled, forming closely knit communities in many cities. Some lived in smaller groups in outlying provincial areas.

Mary and Joseph soon would have discovered the Jewish settlement in Heliopolis, a city in lower Egypt where the delta earth was enriched with silt each year when the floodwaters of the Nile receded. Here, in the city of the sun god, legend claims the holy family found asylum. There is no way, however, to prove this story is based on truth.

Heliopolis Jews wore Greek dress and spoke Greek rather than the familiar Aramaic, but in the outlying region Greek influence was not as strong. Jews settling there had adopted more local Egyptian customs. They tried, as well, to obey the laws of their own religion. Mary and Joseph would have found this to be comforting. No matter how Hellenized Egyptian Jews seemed, they never forgot to send their annual taxes to the Temple in Jerusalem. And the lives of most of the brethren were regulated by the old Jewish calendar and the Sabbath laws.

Egyptian Jews were excused from emperor worship and from paying the taxes raised in support of civic rites. What a relief it must have been for Mary and Joseph to hear this! By paying these taxes they would have honored the city's gods instead of the holy God of Israel. They must have been happy, too, when friends reassured them they would not be forced to attend court on the Sabbath and that Joseph would not be conscripted to serve in the army. Egyptians were tolerant of the fact that Jews could not bear arms on the Sabbath, although Jewish mercenaries took exception to this rule.

As at home, Jews in Egypt gathered at their local synagogues, using the same place for political assemblies, prayers, the singing of psalms, and religious instruction.

If Mary and Joseph remained in this area for any length of time, they may have visited the Jewish temple built years before by Onias IV, the son of a high priest at the Jerusalem Temple. Onias IV had erected his temple on the ruins of an ancient Egyptian temple at Leontopolus, which was in the district of Heliopolis. It has been described as a tower surrounded by a wall. While Egyptian Jews offered sacrifices at this temple, they did not let it replace the Temple in Jerusalem. The sacrifices offered here were not considered idolatrous, but the priests who served here could not also serve in the Jerusalem Temple.

From a distance, Mary and Joseph would have looked with awe at the city villas of upper-class families. Most of their time would have been spent in a peasant home constructed of sun-dried bricks, a house much like the little one they owned in Nazareth except for one thing. Egyptians knew how to strengthen their bricks with straw. For this reason, and also because of the nature of the alluvial mud of the Nile, Egyptian bricks were to last far longer than those used in Palestine.

The holy family would have eaten in their accustomed manner, seated on the floor and dipping from a common dish. Mary would have been entranced, though, at the array of bowls and basins she could choose from whenever she prepared her family's meals. The poorest Egyptian seemed able to afford such bowls, and a number of carved drinking goblets, too.

And what a variety of fruits and vegetables! She found the usual pomegranates, figs, dates, grapes. But who among her friends at home would believe the occasional luxury of a delicious coconut? The markets and the gardens of new friends contained onions, leeks, beans, lentils, radishes, turnips, spinach, garlic, carrots, cucumbers, lettuce, and melons.

The market offered many kinds of bread. Mary would have been delighted at the variety. Most of the time she may have served the familiar stew and other dishes they were accustomed to eating. But perhaps out of curiosity she tried some of the new foods.

Butter and cheese and eggs of all sorts of birds were easy to come by. The Egyptians, especially the wealthier ones, consumed quantities of meat — beef, lamb, goat, and fowl, the latter coming from both wild and domestic birds, including geese, quail, crane, pigeon, and duck. Pork was considered unclean in Egypt as well as in the Jewish homes of Palestine.

At home Mary and Joseph had sometimes roasted a bird upon a spit, but meat had been served only on feast days. Here in Egypt the peasants did not eat meat as frequently as they ate fish. Their taboos about fish were different from those of the ancient Hebrew law which forbade the eating of any creature without scale or fin such as crab or shark. Mary would have continued to observe another Hebrew law, the one stating that meat and fish must be cooked in separate vessels.

The fabulous life under the Pharaohs was over. Egypt had faced the conquering Assyrians, the Persians, and Hellenistic domination during the time of Alexander the Great, and now the Romans. But Mary and Joseph saw the remnants of the past ages of glory — obelisks, pyramids, palaces, and temples. They saw ornate sculptures and intricately carved and painted friezes.

Grand approach to the Temple of Philae

A carpenter looking for work in a strange land, Joseph would have been intrigued by the craftsmanship of Egyptians trained in his trade. During his stay he undoubtedly picked up a few tricks about mitering and graining and veneering wood to try when he returned to his shop in Nazareth.

If the family remained in the delta area, they would have been deeply affected by the Nile River. The long, green strip on either side was very fertile. During a certain season each year it was under floodwaters. The three seasons, all governed by the Nile River, were the Season of the Flood between June and October, the Season of the Going Out when the flood subsided and the farmers hurried to plant their crops, and the Season of the Harvest. If the flood was too great or too small, crops would fail.

Perhaps Mary and Joseph carried Jesus down to the river to watch the passing boats. The larger ones had curved prows and high sterns, and often both were curled into the shape of a papyrus flower. The mast was in the center of the boat. The sail was wide and very long. The boats usually had awnings for protection

The island of Philae on the Nile

against the scorching sun. The rowers knelt on the deck in two rows, facing the stern and plying their curved broad-bladed oars with a steady rhythm.

A group of Egyptians

Overleaf: The Isaiah scroll, one of the Dead Sea Scrolls from Qumran Cave

Life was not always tranquil in Egypt. There were riots and uprisings. Now that Roman citizens were privileged, there was a wave of anti-Semitism. Mary and Joseph must have felt the effects of it at times.

Some wealthy Jews were highly thought of as poets, historians, apologists, philosophers. Philo was numbered among them. But Augustus had disbanded the Ptolemaic army and had abolished the former tax collection system. The brunt of the poll tax fell heavily on the peasantry, and with them, the Jewish residents. Jews who had made a living as tax collectors were replaced. Augustus revised the constitution of Egypt, demoting those who had previously received Greek citizenship.

Relieved though they were to escape Herod's wild murder spree, Mary and Joseph probably longed for the familiar surroundings of home. Some Egyptian ways were difficult to understand. The people worshiped many gods, for instance. A man was permitted to have several wives. Brothers and sisters were allowed to marry each other. The sacred Jewish Scriptures spoke so clearly against this that Mary and Joseph would have been shocked. They must have felt revolted, too, by the equally common custom of leaving an unwanted baby on a dunghill to die. One law stated that any Egyptian who rescued such a baby and reared him as his child must surrender a quarter of his estate to the state at death. A father also had a right to sell his child.

Joseph and Mary had so much to look at and absorb, so many new ideas to mull over. There were fascinating luxuries such as coconuts, perfumes, trinkets of gold and ivory. And they made new friends in the community where they settled. Yet, as soon as the angel appeared in Joseph's dream one night, they were ready to go home to their hilly province of Galilee. That was where they belonged. And that was where they wanted to rear their child.

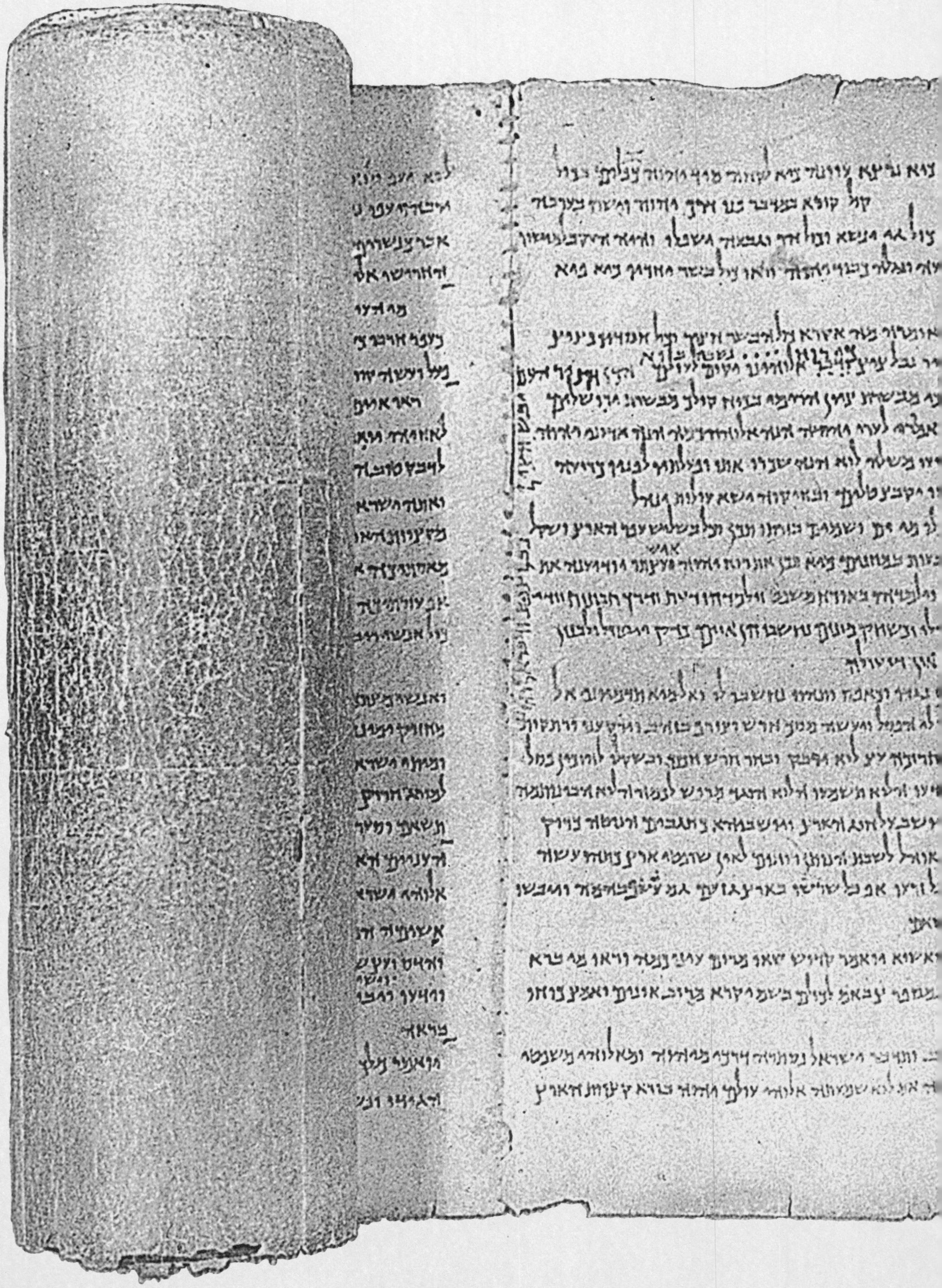

AT HOME IN NAZARETH

"And the child grew and became strong, filled with wisdom; and the favor of God was upon him." Luke 2:40

Mary and Joseph may have taken another route home, journeying along the seacoast to Gaza, past Caesarea, and around the foot of Mt. Carmel. They gave Judea a wide berth because they had heard that Herod's son, Archelaus, was the new ruler. On this route they would have crossed the Kishon and reached, at last, the foothills of Galilee.

The Bible leaves out many details. Did Mary wonder, for instance, what they would find when they reached Nazareth? Would Joseph's home and shop be intact?

"Yes, yes," one can almost hear him reassure her. "My neighbors promised to take care of any emergency."

Mary might have wistfully replied, "But they did not know we would be gone so long. Perhaps by now no one expects us to come home again."

After they re-entered the Holy Land, Mary and Joseph would have undergone a ritual purification lasting seven days. People coming from a foreign country were considered unclean.

And then, when they climbed through the hills and the high valley to Nazareth, what a warm welcome must have awaited them! There were changes. Some friends and relatives had moved away; others had died in their absence. But surely they were greeted with joy and with exclamations over their strong, healthy little son. No one knows how old Jesus was at this time.

In the following years the family grew. The Bible lists at least four brothers and several sisters. The brothers are named in the books of Matthew and Mark (Judas, James, Joseph, and Simeon) but the sisters are not. At times it has been suggested that Joseph was a widower and these might have been his offspring by a former marriage. There is no historical basis for this claim. Possibly the

Left: Mount Carmel

children were Jesus' cousins. In Bible days often the word *brother* referred to cousins and nephews, and extended families were common.

The children tussled and fought as all children do, played tag and blindman's bluff, skinned their knees, ran races, raised pet lambs and goats, and hiked into the hills to hunt for pretty stones and flowers and bird eggs.

Later Jesus would speak of the way children imitated funerals and weddings, piping notes on the crude reed pipes they made with their own hands. As a youngster he must have done these things himself. He and his brothers and sisters and cousins laughed and shouted and played, and sometimes they wept.

While his sisters helped Mary grind the grain and bake the flat rounds of bread, while they learned how to spin and weave and do other household tasks, Jesus and his brothers would have assisted Joseph in the shop.

With a chip of wood tucked behind his ear as a badge of his craft, Joseph would have taught Jesus the proper way to hold a beam between his toes, to measure for a door lintel, to make a kneading trough, and, of course, how to use the ax and saw and adz safely.

Many times Joseph may have had to call Jesus home from play to help him carry the materials for a new roof through the narrow streets, and also to help with construction.

If the family owned a goat or two or a couple of sheep, Jesus and his brothers would have had to drive the animals out to the hills to find good grazing spots. At night they probably took turns milking the animals, carefully separating into different containers the goats' milk and sheep's milk.

The houses were built so close together that most people planted their gardens on the edge of town. There, in Joseph's plot, Jesus and his brothers may have knelt to weed the cucumbers and the beans and onions.

During the olive harvest, parents and children joined in beating fruit from the trees with a long stick. Everyone helped carry loads of fruit from the trees to the waiting press. The time of the grape harvest was one of rejoicing with songs and dances and the telling of old folktales. And shearing time was fun too!

The synagogue was the pivot of village life. The faithful who were able went there daily to face Jerusalem and recite the *Shema.* Civic affairs as well as religious ones were carried on at the synagogue. Leaders attended to the community's affairs there.

At the synagogue, there may have been a small school for boys about six years of age. They sat on the floor in a semicircle around the teacher. They memorized passages of Scripture and learned by heart the stories of Abraham, Isaac, Jacob, and the prophets and

Children on the floor, rocking themselves to and fro, while reciting their lessons

kings. They had heard these stories countless times before during family gatherings at night on the rooftops.

Daily Jesus spoke Aramaic. If he had an opportunity to attend a primary school at the synagogue, he would have learned Hebrew there. On the Sabbath, at synagogue, the reader of the Hebrew text spontaneously paraphrased it in Aramaic. Luke relates how Jesus himself did this when he visited his home synagogue in Nazareth as an adult. We know from this reference that he was able to read Hebrew and it is likely that he spoke it too.

The people of Palestine were not as time-conscious as we are today. The only day of the week to possess a name was the Sabbath, our Saturday. The seven-day period of a week was measured by counting the days between two Sabbaths.

The natural day began at dawn when the family chanted the *Shema Yisrael,* and it ended at dusk. But legally one day ended and the next began at the hour of sunset.

Apparently the Jews did not have any clocks similar to the Roman sundial or waterclock. The New Testament does speak of events taking place "at the sixth hour" or "at the ninth hour," indicating that by the time Jesus was growing up the days were thought of as 12-hour periods of time. The nights had long been divided into four watches: the evening watch, the midnight watch, the cockcrow watch, and the dawn watch.

Religious rituals were very much a part of Jesus' boyhood experience. Daily he joined his family in reciting the *Shema Yisrael.* Like women, boys were excused from taking part in this ritual until they were 13 years of age, but Jesus would have memorized the prayer as a small child. As a little boy, too, he would have watched his father strap the phylacteries onto his arm and forehead after repeating special prayers, when he was about to worship the God of Israel.

First century oil lamp

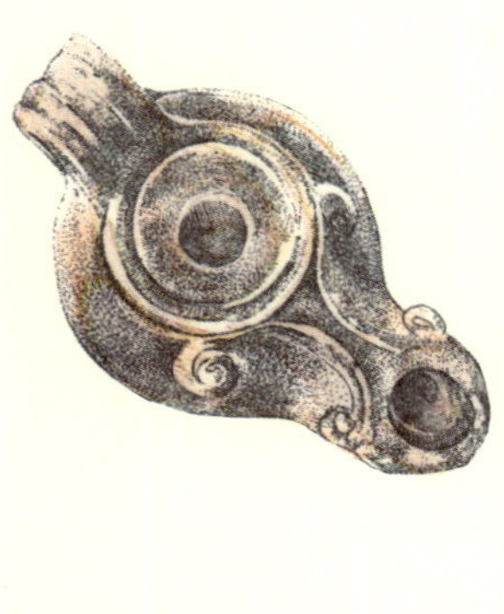

Each time food was eaten there was a ritual washing of hands, and a blessing afterwards. Weekly, Jesus would have watched with interest as Mary and his sisters cleaned the house and prepared all the food they would need for the Sabbath day when no cooking would be done.

The eve of the Sabbath was a dignified, quiet time. Legally it began about an hour before the first three stars could be seen in the night sky. Work ceased. It was time for the Sabbath lamp to be lit in every home. As the mother of the family, Mary was the guardian of this lamp. She made sure it was clean and filled with fresh oil each week.

After washing carefully, the family sat down to share a special Sabbath meal, including wine and herbs blessed with a threefold prayer. They would not eat again until they had attended services at the synagogue the following morning. A hungry boy might have had many questions about this custom!

Until the age of 12, Jesus joined his mother and sisters in the place reserved for women and children at the synagogue. As a child he would have sniffed the fresh, minty smell as people trod upon the herb-strewn floor and took their places. The elders and other important townspeople had the chief seats. Others sat in order of their trades. Nearest the pulpit were the skilled artisans, the silversmiths and tailors and sandalmakers. Farther back were the bakers and dyers and cheesemakers. Along the walls sat the rest of the tradesmen and farmers.

After the Scripture had been read in Hebrew and paraphrased in Aramaic by the reader, the passage was discussed. Sometimes in the afternoon people would return to the synagogue for a further discussion of the Law.

With the appearance of stars, when the Sabbath was over, Jesus' family gathered for supper, after first blessing the light and the wine and herbs three times. When the meal was finished the members of the family would rise, wash their hands once again, and give thanks over a goblet of wine passed around and shared. The haunting beauty of the Sabbath ritual would have left a deep

The requisite "four kinds of plants" (willow, palm, myrtle, and citron) used during the Feast of Tabernacles, one of the three great feasts for which pilgrims journeyed to Jerusalem. Crowds went up to the Temple holding the "four spices," singing and dancing.

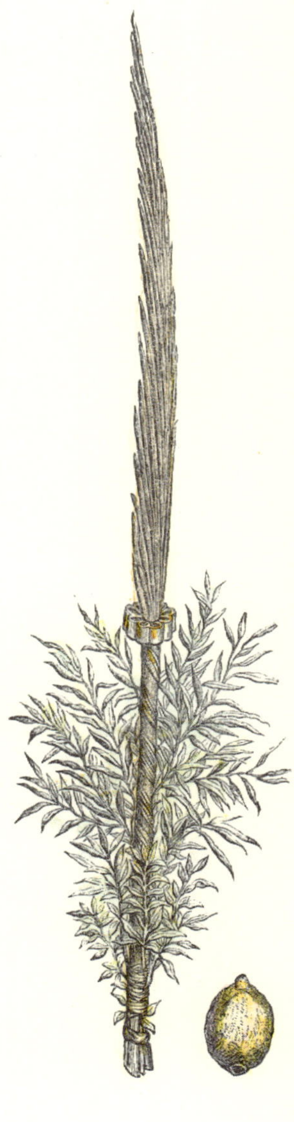

Various forms of tabernacles

impression on Jesus. But like other children, he was probably glad when he was allowed to run and play after it was done!

Each year the family looked forward to the Feast of Passover, the Feast of Pentecost, and the Feast of Tabernacles. There were other feasts too, and celebrations at the time of shearing and the village weddings.

Passover recalled the escape of the Hebrews from Egyptian bondage. There was always a flurry of preparation — housecleaning and baking unleavened bread. Joseph had to make a ceremonial search on the eve of the feast to rid the cleaned home of the tiniest crumb of leavened bread or dough. Then began the great feast.

Often the family may have made a pilgrimage to Jerusalem for the Passover. The Holy City overflowed with visitors each year. Joseph would have chosen an unblemished yearling lamb to give as a sacrifice. After the lamb had been slaughtered and the priest had poured its blood on the altar, the entrails and fat were tossed into the fire and the sacrificed lamb was eaten by the family at a ritual meal.

But first, before feasting on the roasted lamb, the family dipped unleavened bread in a red sauce and sipped blessed wine, reciting a psalm. They drank drops of salt water to remind themselves of the tears their ancestors had shed. With the lamb, bitter herbs were eaten, and more wine was passed in a special ritual.

Pentecost, celebrated after the grain had been harvested, was not only a harvest feast but a religious celebration recalling the giving of the Law to Moses.

Perhaps the feast Jesus loved best as a child was the Feast of Tabernacles or Ingathering held every October. This thank-offering to God for the harvest also was a memorial of the years the Chosen People had wandered in the wilderness. For a whole week everyone slept outside in little tent-houses constructed from boughs with the leaves plaited to form the roof and sides of the

Bringing the first fruits as offering to the Temple

tent. Some families built their tent-house in their courtyard, beneath a fig or an olive tree. Many were built on the flat rooftops. Jesus and his friends could race from rooftop to rooftop, admiring each others' tent-houses!

If he traveled with his family to Jerusalem to celebrate this feast, Jesus sometimes would have noticed how the dry weather had parched the land. Everyone longed for rain to come. There would be prayers for rain when they reached the Temple.

Pilgrims coming from distant places proceeded into the city singing verses from the Psalms, and some played accompaniment on pipes. After the priests came out to meet the throng, they continued to the gates of the Temple, carrying their harvest gifts, baskets of corn and fruit. Jesus may have been one of the eager boys who carried a couple of doves or pigeons.

At night when the lamps of the Temple were lit, there was singing and the music of many beautiful instruments — harps and trumpets, cymbals and pipes. All of it would echo in a small boy's mind for months to come.

Musical instruments played by the priests in the Temple: *shofar* (ram's horn), timbrels, trumpets, and harp *(overleaf)*.

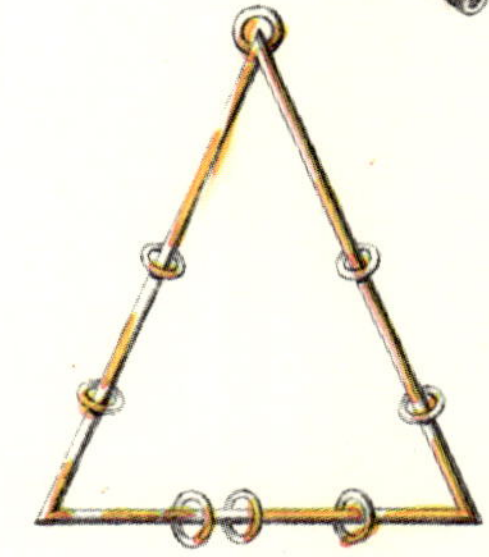

We know what life was like at that time for a Jewish family living in Palestine. But the Bible gives no details of Jesus' childhood and we cannot fill in the gaps. When she was alone with her son, did Mary try to prepare him for what was to come by telling him of the angel's visit or of Simeon's words? Did she ever unwrap the gifts brought by the Wise Men so Jesus might get a glimmer of the importance of his birth?

Our questions must go unanswered. Perhaps Jesus' own probing questions — the ones he asked of the learned doctors, even as a young boy — made him sense his destiny.

The Holy Land, a tiny area in the Mideast, is the place where Christmas happened. But the message the angels sang 2000 years ago can be heard again today. Emmanuel, Emmanuel, God is with us!

Whenever he is born within a human heart — that, too, is the land of Christmas!

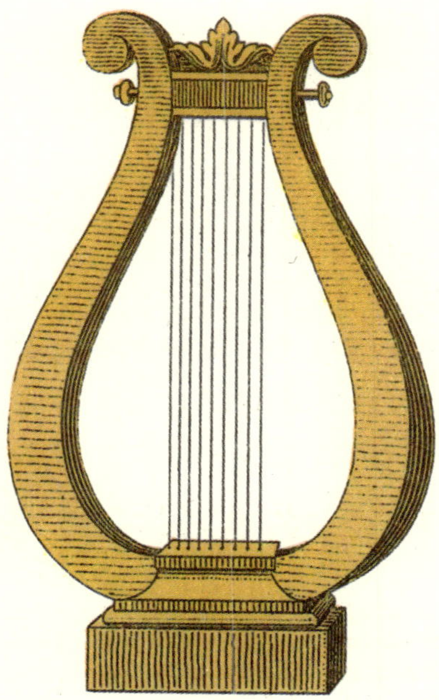

Sources for the Illustrations

The Land of Christmas is profusely illustrated by a choice selection of lithographs, wood and steel engravings, and drawings of nineteenth century artists, some well known, others whose works were discovered by scholars and used to illustrate books about the Holy Land more than a century ago.
Numbers below refer to pages in this book.

Walks about the City and Environs of Jerusalem by W.H. Bartlett. Published by George Virtue, London, 1844.
The Christians in Palestine — or Scenes of Sacred History, Historical and Descriptive by Henry Stebbing D.D., F.R.S. Illustrated from sketches taken on the spot by W.H. Bartlett. Published by George Virtue, London, 1847.

William Henry Bartlett (1809-1855), an English landscape painter famous for his artistic and informative travel illustrations, depicted scenes of his native England, Europe, America, and the Middle East, including two travelogs about Jerusalem. His delicate line drawings of the Holy Land show sharp insight and wide knowledge of historical and topographical research. The drawings of his first voyage to the Holy Land in 1835 were used to illustrate the three volumes of *Syria, the Holy Land, Asia Minor,* by J. Crane (1835). Other books of his are: *The Christian in Palestine (1847), Forty Days in the Desert (1848), Scripture Sites and Scenes (1851), and Jerusalem Revisited (1855).*

pp. 2-3, 20-21, 31, 32-33, 40-41, 42, 50-51, 61, 63, 68-69, 82-83, 86.

The Life of Christ by Frederic W. Farrar D.D., F.R.S. Published by Cassel, Petter & Galpin, London, 1870.

Born in the Fort of Bombay in 1831, Farrar became teacher, author, and one of England's leading clerics. His *Life of Christ* had a large number of editions. His *Life and Works of St. Paul* and *The Early Days of Christianity* were also popular. After an appointment as Chaplin-in-Ordinary to Queen Victoria, he became Canon of Westminster and Dean of Canterbury.

pp. 16, 17, 22, 44, 45, 46, 47, 49, 84, 115, 116.

Landscape Illustrations of the Bible engraved by W. and E. Finden. Published in two volumes by John Murray, London, 1836.

William Finden (1787-1852) and his younger brother Edward were English line engravers. Their neat style, superb craftsmanship, and smooth finish made their prints very popular in England and abroad. One of their most successful productions was the book of biblical landscapes. Sketches and notes taken by travelers on the spot were redrawn by prominent British artists such as D. Roberts (see below) and J.M.W. Turner. Turner (1775-1851), today considered England's foremost romantic painter and most original landscape artist, drew the view of Bethlehem from sketches made by C. Barry and Rev. R. Master.

p.19

The Pictorial History of Palestine and the Holy Land by John Kitto. Published by Charles Knight & Co., London, 1844.

John Kitto (1804-1854) was a leading biblical scholar. While traveling in the Holy Land, Kitto obtained personal knowledge of oriental life and habits. Upon his return to England in 1832, he applied these experiences with great skill to illustrations of biblical scenes and incidents. His first major work, *Palestine: The Physical Geography and Natural History of the Holy Land,* was published in 1841, followed later by other books on the Bible.

pp. 36, 37, 52, 56, 78. 117.

L'univers-Palestine ou Histoire et Description de tous les peuples de leurs religions, Moeurs, Costumes. Description Géographique, Historique et Archéologique by S. Munk. Firmin Didot Frères, editeurs, Paris, 1841.

Solomon Munk (1803-1867), French Orientalist, born in Silesia, studied in a rabbinical school and in the Universities of Bonn and Berlin. In 1828 he was made head of the Semitic Manuscripts Department at Bibliothèque Nationale, in Paris. He visited the Middle East in 1840, collecting manuscripts and implements used in the East. In 1864, Munk, a professor of Hebrew and Syriac literature was elected a member of the Academie Française.

pp. 30, 92, 93, 94, 117, 118.

The Holy Land from drawings made on location by David Roberts, .R.A. with historical description by the Rev. George Croly L.L.D. Drawn on stone by Louis Haghe for Day & Son, lithographers to the Queen, London, 1842-1849.

David Roberts (1796-1864) received the ultimate recognition as an artist following his career as a stage designer for the theater. The enthusiastic acclaim of his first biblical landscape, "Departure of the Israelites from Egypt," allowed him to leave the theater. In 1837 a selection of his drawings from Spain was reproduced by lithography. A year later, Roberts left for a long tour to the East, spending the next ten years redrawing his sketches into elaborate graphic masterpieces, lithographed and published in three giant volumes. While working on his Holy Land drawings, Roberts was elected member of the Royal Academy.

pp. 64-65, 102, 105, 107.

Le Temple de Jerusalem, Monographie du Haram-Ech-cherif by Comte Melchior de Vogüé, Noblet & Baudry, Paris, 1864.

Charles Eugene Melchior Comte de Vogüé (1829-1916) was a French architect and archeologist. During his research expedition to the Holy Land in 1853-4, De Vogüé studied and sketched the Temple enclosure and made important discoveries in the history of Roman and Byzantine architecture. In 1871 he was appointed French ambassador to Constantinople and later to Vienna.

p. 95

Picturesque Palestine, Sinai and Egypt edited by Sir Charles W. Wilson K.C.B., D.C.L., F.R.S., R.E. Published by Virtue & Co., London, 1880.

Sir Charles William Wilson (1836-1905) joined the Royal Engineers at the age of 19. During his extensive work in Jerusalem he discovered at the Western Wall an arch of a bridge that connected the Second Temple and the Upper City. It was named Wilson's Arch in his honor and described in his book *The Recovery of Jerusalem* written with C. Warren (1871). In 1880 Wilson wrote and edited three volumes of *Picturesque Palestine* and one volume of *Sinai and Egypt*, all composed of studies by eminent explorers, using many wood and steel engravings drawn by various artists.

pp. 8-9, 13, 14, 15, 25, 29, 34, 55, 57, 58-59, 66, 71, 72-73, 74, 76, 77, 81, 96-97, 98, 101, 103, 106, 110, 113.

Drawings of archeological finds by:

M. Gabrieli: pp. 38, 79, 91, 108-109;
Sara Halbreich: pp. 26, 27, 30, 53, 114.

Bibliography

Aharoni, Yohanan. **The Land of the Bible.** Philadelphia: Westminster, 1967.
Albright, W.F. **Archeology of Palestine.** New York: Penguin, 1960.
Baly, Denis. **The Geography of the Bible.** New York: Harper, 1974.
Bonsirvan, J. **Palestinian Judaism in the Time of Jesus Christ.** New York: Holt, Rinehart, and Winston, 1964.
Bouquet, A.C. **Everyday Life in New Testament Times.** New York: Scribners, 1953.
Comay, Joan. **The Temple of Jerusalem.** New York: Holt, Rinehart, and Winston, 1975.
Dana, H.E. **The New Testament World.** Nashville: Broadman, 1941.
Daniel-Rops, H. **Daily Life in the Time of Jesus.** New York: Hawthorne, 1962.
Daniel-Rops, H. **The Life of Our Lord.** New York: Hawthorne, 1964.
Entwistle, Mary. **The Bible Guidebook.** Nashville: Abingdon, 1952.
Farb, Peter. **The Land, Wildlife, and Peoples of the Bible.** New York: Harper, 1967.
Glueck, Nelson. **The River Jordan.** Philadelphia: Westminster, 1946.
Goodspeed, Edgar. **A Life of Jesus.** New York: Harper, 1950.
Gromacki, Robert G. **New Testament Survey.** Grand Rapids, Mich.: Baker, 1974.
Guignebert, Charles. **The Jewish World in the Time of Jesus.** New York: Dutton, 1939.
Hastings, James, ed. **Dictionary of the Bible.** New York: Scribners, 1961.
Hausrath, Adolf. **Time of Jesus, History of the New Testament Times.** London: William and Norgate, 1878.
Henderson and Gould. **Life in Bible Times.** Chicago: Rand McNally, 1967.
Holmgren, Virginia. **Birdwalk Through the Bible.** New York: Seabury, 1972.
Interpreters Bible Commentaries. Nashville: Abingdon, 1952.
Jeremias, Joachim. **Jerusalem in the Time of Jesus.** Philadelphia: Fortress, 1969.
Johnson, Sherman. **Jesus in His Homeland.** New York: Scribners, 1957.
Jones, Clifford. **New Testament Illustrations.** New York: Cambridge Univ. Press, 1966.
Keys, Nelson. **Story of the Bible World.** Maplewood, New York: Hammond, 1959.
Klausner, Joseph. **Jesus of Nazareth, His Life, Times and Teaching.** New York: Macmillan, 1926.
Kopp, Clemens. **The Holy Places of the Gospels.** London: Herder and Herder, 1963.
Kotker, ed. **The Holy Land in the Time of Jesus.** New York: Horizon, 1955.
Kraeling. **Rand McNally Bible Atlas.** Chicago: Rand McNally, 1956.
Leary, L.G. **The Christmas City.** New York: Sturgis Walton, 1911.
Legendre. **The Cradle of the Bible.** London: Sands and Co., 1930.
Lessing, Erich. **Jesus: History and Culture of the New Testament.** London; St. Louis: Herder and Herder, 1971.
MacCoun, Townsend. **Holy Land in Geography and in History.** New York, 1897.
Mackie, George M. **Bible Manners and Customs.** Old Tappan, N.J.: Fleming Revell, 1898.
Matthews, B.J. **The World in Which Jesus Lived.** Nashville: Abingdon, 1938.
Miller, Madeleine; Miller, J. Lane. **Encyclopedia of Bible Life.** New York: Harper, 1944.
Miller, Madeleine; Miller, J. Lane. **Harper Dictionary of the Bible.** New York: Harper, 1973.
Morton, H.V. **Through Lands of the Bible.** New York: Dodd Mead, 1938.
National Geographic Society. **Everyday Life in Bible Times.** Washington D.C.: 1967.
Noth, Martin. **The History of Israel.** New York: Harper, 1960.
Parrot, Andre. **The Temple of Jerusalem.** New York: Philosophical Society, 1955.
Patai, Raphael. **Tents of Jacob.** Englewood, N.J.: Prentice Hall, 1971.
Perowne, Stewart. **The Life and Times of Herod the Great.** Nashville: Abingdon, n.d.
Perowne, Stewart. **Jerusalem and Bethlehem Guidebooks.** London: Phoenix House, 1965.
Prat, Ferdinand. **Jesus Christ, His Life, His Teachings, and His Work.** Milwaukee: Bruce, 1950.
Rand, Christopher. **Christmas in Bethlehem.** New York: Oxford Univ. Press, 1963.
Reicke, Bo Ivar. **The New Testament Era.** Philadelphia: Fortress, 1974.
Riccotti. **Life of Christ.** Milwaukee: Bruce Publishing Co., 1948.
Roth, Cecil. **A History of the Jews.** New York: Schocken Books, 1970.
Schauss, Hayyim. **The Lifetime of a Jew.** New York: Schocken Books, 1954.
Schurer, Emil. **A History of the Jewish People in the Time of Jesus.** New York: Schocken Books, 1961.
Sharp, Della. **Christ and His Time.** Nashville: Abingdon, 1933.
Silver, Daniel Jeremy. **A History of Judaism,** Vol. I. New York: Basic Books, 1974.
Smith, George Adam. **The Historical Geography of the Holy Land.** New York: Harper and Row, 1966.
Vaart Smit, H.W. van der. **Born in Bethlehem: Christmas As It Really Was.** Baltimore: Helicon, 1963.
Walker, Winifred. **All the Plants of the Bible.** New York: Harper, 1957.
Williams, Albert. **The Holy City.** New York: Duell Sloan and Pearce, 1954.
Wright, G.E. **The Westminster Historical Atlas.** Philadelphia: Westminster, 1956.
Encyclopaedia Judaica. Jerusalem: Keter, 1972.